UK Political Parties
Since 1945

CONTEMPORARY POLITICAL STUDIES

Series Editor: John Benyon, *University of Leicester*

A series which provides authoritative and concise introductory accounts
of key topics in contemporary political studies

CONTEMPORARY POLITICAL STUDIES

UK Political Parties Since 1945

Edited by

ANTHONY SELDON
Institute of Contemporary British History

Assisted by Gerard Daly

Philip Allan
NEW YORK LONDON TORONTO SYDNEY TOKYO SINGAPORE

First published 1990 by
Philip Allan
66 Wood Lane End, Hemel Hempstead
Hertfordshire, HP2 4RG
A division of
Simon & Schuster International Group

Printed and bound in Great Britain by
Billing and Sons Ltd, Worcester

British Library Cataloguing in Publication Data

UK political parties since 1945. – (Contemporary
    political studies)
    1. Great Britain. Political parties, history
    I. Seldon, Anthony II. The Contemporary Record III.
Series
324.241'009

ISBN 0–86003–410–0

2 3 4 5 94 93 92 91 90

Contents

Contributors

Paul Arthur is Lecturer in Politics at the University of Ulster and author of several books on Northern Ireland, including *Northern Ireland since 1968* (with Keith Jeffery, Blackwell/ICBH, 1988).

John Callaghan is Senior Lecturer in Politics at Wolverhampton Polytechnic. He is author of *The Far Left in British Politics* (Blackwell, 1988).

Gerard Daly is a doctoral research student at Birkbeck College, London.

James Kellas is Professor in Politics at the University of Glasgow.

Kenneth O. Morgan, formerly Fellow of The Queen's College, Oxford, is Principal of the University College of Wales, Aberystwyth. His many books include *Labour in Power, 1945–51* (OUP, 1984) and *Labour People: Leaders and Lieutenants, Hardie to Kinnock* (new pbk edn 1989). His history of Britain from 1945 to 1989 will be published in 1990.

Gillian Peele is a Fellow of Lady Margaret Hall, Oxford, and tutor in Politics. Her latest book is on political parties in Britain, to be published by Philip Allan.

Michael Pinto-Duschinsky is Senior Lecturer in Government at Brunel University. He is Vice-Chairman of the International

Political Science Association's research committee on political finance and corruption.

John Ramsden is Senior Reader at Queen Mary College, London. His books include *The Making of Conservative Policy* (Longman, 1988).

Alan Ryan has been a Fellow of New College, Oxford, and is currently at Princeton University.

John Stevenson is Reader in History at the University of Sheffield and is author of *British Society 1914–45* (Penguin, 1984).

Introduction

This book consists of ten essays, many by leading authorities in their field. The uniting theme is the determination to view parties in their recent historical setting. Because all parties, and not just the two principal national parties, have undergone such profound changes since 1945, an understanding of postwar developments is essential to a full appreciation of contemporary realities.

The chapters are mostly concerned with particular parties, both national and regional. The chapter on the Northern Ireland party system is particularly important because a consideration of it is so often lacking in books on politics. Two chapters concern themselves with themes: one with party ideology, the other with party finance. Internal party organisation and democracy is a crucial theme, but not one which the editor believes merits a separate chapter because the subject is discussed in the chapters on the parties.

Each author writes in his own particular style, and focuses on issues he or she believes important. Beyond some bare guidelines, the editor did not impose common themes. To have done so might have made for a more regimented book, but it would have been at the cost of losing these authors' particular flavours and approaches.

The chapters have already appeared, or will do so, in the pages of *Contemporary Record,* the quarterly journal of the Institute of Contemporary British History. It was the conviction of the editor that the chapters deserved a wider audience.

Anthony Seldon

1

The Labour Party Since 1945

KENNETH O. MORGAN

Commentators on British politics in the eighties invariably focus on Labour's contraction, both in electoral support and intellectual fire-power. Indeed, the decline of the Labour Party seems as much a part of the conventional wisdom as was the decline of the Liberals (not to mention the rise of the gentry) in earlier times. Yet it is only since 1945 that Labour has been a significant, consistent challenger for power. In the first three decades of its existence, ever since its foundation in 1900, Labour was an inchoate alliance of trade unionists, socialists and freelance radicals, with neither clear objectives nor a coherent structure. The first two Labour governments of 1924 and 1929 were both minority affairs, dependent on Liberal support. A promising Labour upsurge after the general strike was killed off by the financial crash of 1931. Throughout the thirties, Labour was engaged in an uphill process of recovery. Had there been a general election in 1939 or 1940, the party still believed it would have been comfortably defeated by Neville Chamberlain, as the alleged architect of prosperity and peace.

It is, of course, the Attlee ministry of 1945–51 which is the launch-pad of Labour's modern history. Only since then has it been a party geared to government. The legend of 1945 is still central to the ideas and illusions of the British variant of democratic

1

socialism. It keeps the flame alive. It symbolises a unique historic moment of Labour in power, mobilised purposively for dynamic action and social change. Its appeal extends right across the party spectrum. Benn on the left can hail it as a victory for socialism and near-revolutionary advance; Hattersley on the right can extol the 'sensible', broad-church reformism of Attlee and his comrades. And 1945, too, symbolises a year of victory over fascism. Labour was as central to winning the war as the titanic figure of Churchill himself. For once, the British left can play the patriotic card.

But of course, the landslide victory of 1945 was a product of far more profound forces. It was the indirect legacy of the intellectual revival of British socialism in the late thirties, when Labour appropriated the idea of planning for its own Fabian purposes, and also acquired a credible foreign policy for the first time. And the party's 1945 victory would have been inconceivable without the change of mood created during the war years, the new enthusiasm for planning and social engineering, the passion for equality and reconstruction. Especially among the professional classes and the intelligentsia was this rare urge for reform apparent – even in the deepest recesses of the Treasury, even amongst traditionally élitist occupations like doctors and architects. This all created a unique skein of circumstances vital to the purposes of the left. They were not to be repeated.

The Attlee years: coherence of party and policies

There are ample grounds for supposing that the Attlee government was successful, competent and frequently creative. There is also reason to argue that its achievements rested on a series of factors coincidentally embedded in the psyche of the movement, in a way and to a degree that could not arise again. First, the Attlee government, far more so than any other Labour administration, was united and cohesive to an unusual and impressive extent. It was led from the top, by unassailably powerful figures like Attlee himself, Bevin as the voice of the unions, and Morrison as orchestrator of the party machine, to be joined later by the powerful managerial presence of Cripps. This was a secure leadership under no challenge from within. Party morale was generally high, despite the travails of postwar austerity. Membership kept on rising. Every by-election where Labour was defending a seat (save for one freak result in Glasgow) was victoriously contested. This united mood was underpinned by a second feature of the Attlee years – the structural coherence of party and movement. Labour is a notoriously ungovernable body of comrades with a supremely cumbersome hybrid constitution. In 1945–51, though, it all seemed comparatively streamlined. The parliamentary party, for all its huge membership of 394 MPs, was generally loyalist, its flights of rebellion muted and seldom damaging. The NEC was dominated by Cabinet ministers like Morrison and Dalton, with their trade union allies. Party conference was a forum for triumphalist appearance by the leader before his fighting legions; it was more docile after 1945 than ever before or since. Transport House, under the resourceful direction of Morgan Phillips, was a solid organisational prop for the leadership. Most important of all, the TUC, under the famous right-wing troika of Deakin, Williamson and Lawther, saw its main role as lending solid support to the government. In such difficult passages as the imposition of the wage freeze in 1948, this sustaining of the leadership by the unions was essential in keeping Attlee's team buoyant and secure.

The other dominant feature of Attlee's government was the rare certainty of its policy priorities. The party manifesto in 1945 set out with clarity what it intended to do; with few exceptions, this agenda of reform was duly implemented. Nationalisation of over 20 per cent of the economy went through, for staples like coal, services like road and rail transport, gas and electricity, the Bank of England, and, far more controversially, iron and steel. The disputes over this last heralded the later erosion of support for public ownership; but in 1945–51 a finite programme of nationalisation commanded broad acceptance. So, emphatically, did the implementation of the Welfare State, which by 1950 Labour largely claimed as its own. Many of its features – social security, education, housing – did not go far, if at all, beyond wartime blueprints. But the Health Service, with all its limitations, did have a clear socialist ring to it; Aneurin Bevan, its architect, acquired a rare charisma as an effective radical executive. Labour's other agreed home priority was full employment. Armed with the controls of wartime and such coalition measures as the 1945 Distribution of Industry Act, Labour's claim to be running a planned economy – implausible in other respects – had tangible proof in a genuine nationwide growth of an expanding export-led economy, and an end to the squalid indignities of the prewar 'depressed areas' policy. And Labour's priorities had overseas implications as well. Attlee in 1945, like another socialist leader, François Mitterrand in 1981, believed axiomatically that his nation was a great power, one of the 'big three', the fulcrum of western Europe and the Atlantic alliance, the Brussels treaty and NATO. In the Commonwealth, while achieving the break-through of the transfer of power for India and Pakistan, Attlee's government acted imperially at the centre of a worldwide fiscal, trading and defence system. Not since Joseph Chamberlain's heyday had the Colonial Office been so vigorous.

The major constraint on this government, of course, was external, the parlous financial condition of the nation in August 1945 which led Keynes to talk in terms of another Dunkirk. Frequent economic crises rocked the government in these six years. The 1947 convertibility crisis (following a coal shortage) saw a huge run on the reserves; the events leading to the 1949 devaluation of the pound were no less disturbing; the balance of payments collapse in 1951, during the Korean War, brought other intimations of mortality. These storms that beset Attlee's team are incontestable. On the other hand, it is notable that economic difficulties did not lead to a reversal of the government's priorities. Even under Cripps's austerity régime in 1948–50, social spending on the Welfare State and food subsidies were kept up; regional policies to promote full employment were still a major priority. Under the spartan Cripps in 1950 as under the extrovert Dalton in 1945, there remained a sense of socialist purpose.

In some ways, of course, this surface picture of unity and coherence is a deceptive one. There are always tensions and frictions within the broad frame of the Labour movement, and 1945–51 was no exception. Trade union disaffection became vocal from 1948, during the wage-freeze era, with frequent unofficial strikes as indications of protest against the edicts of Transport House and a right-led TUC. There were swarms of dissenters in the constituency parties, angry with the failure to introduce socialist measures such as the conscription of wealth, with expelling rebels like Zilliacus, or with the cold war foreign policies of Ernest Bevin. The Labour Party archives for post-1945 reveal to the curious researcher the deftness of Morgan Phillips in sweeping such incidental opposition under the Smith Square carpet. But only in April 1951 did these forces of dissent find any significant force or claim a leader. This came with the resignation of Aneurin Bevan, accompanied by Harold Wilson, from the Attlee Cabinet. Bevan had hitherto been a generally loyalist member of the administration. But a combination of fury at an inflated rearmament programme undertaken at US dictation leading to charges being imposed on his own Health Service, allied with personal resentment at the promotion of the younger Gaitskell to the Exchequer over his head, led to Bevan splitting away. It was a fateful moment, the inauguration in many ways of thirty years of internecine civil war which cost the party dear. On the other hand, the 1951 General Election, which Labour narrowly lost, showed it was still in good fettle. Labour polled more votes than the Tories, more votes than any British party has ever done before or since. In working-class strongholds like the Welsh mining valleys, it won more votes even than in 1945. Certainly, the mere defeat of the Attlee government does not entitle us to proclaim that this was a party in inexorable decline.

1951–63: Labour divided and defeated

The fifties, however, proved to be a highly damaging and divisive time. The thirteen years of Tory rule saw Labour lose three elections running, its leaders torn by a series of bitter and personalised internal feuds. The unity, the structural coherence, the certainty of priorities of the 1945 period abruptly disappeared. After the third defeat in 1959, when Macmillan's Tory government romped home with a majority of one hundred, there were many pessimistic diagnoses of the 'Must Labour Lose?' variety. Attention focused on the affluent worker, deracinated by the consumer prosperity of the fifties, and no longer automatically identified with the solidarity of workshop organisation or the cohesiveness of working-class community life. At the same time, it is important to understand of what precisely these party divisions consisted. In large measure they related to foreign and defence issues; they were Labour's muddled response to the eclipse of external power. In Attlee's final phase, the party tore itself apart over German rearmament and the attitude to American policy in the Far East, especially towards China. These issues were the staples of the Bevanite upsurge in the constituencies and the unions against first Attlee's, then Gaitskell's leadership. Later in the fifties, with Gaitskell and Bevan now formally reconciled in an uneasy partnership, the party split with even greater violence over the rise of CND and Britain's nuclear defence policy, either independently or in alliance with the USA. There was a colossal rift in the party in 1960 with Gaitskell rebuffed by party conference over the bomb, then fighting back with rare ferocity in 1961 to defeat CND in turn.

By contrast, domestic policy provoked much less dissent. In practice, Aneurin Bevan was as committed as was Hugh Gaitskell to the mixed economy and a distinctly revisionist brand of democratic socialism. The defeat of Gaitskell over Clause Four at the post-election party conference in October 1959 may lead the unwary to conclude that Labour was still in some sense a party committed to traditional socialism and public ownership of the commanding heights. But Clause Four was largely a symbolic issue, almost a totem. His defeat was largely a comment on Gaitskell's abrasive and unduly literal approach at this time. There was, in fact, scant evidence that Clause Four cost Labour any votes at all in 1959, or indeed that the voters (save for a handful of pedantic students of the past careers of Henderson or Sidney Webb) even knew what it was. The fluid approach to socialism conveyed in Tony Crosland's *Future of Socialism* in 1956 – its lack of concern with nationalisation or centralisation, its emphasis on the quality of life, social equality and the co-operative ethic – provided the central themes of most Labour thinking on domestic issues at this time. Ex-Bevanites like Wilson and Crossman subscribed to them, too; Bevan himself had never really been a Bevanite anyway. This revisionist form of socialism, Bad Godesberg-style, thus became the kernel of the party's new approach in the early sixties. It was endorsed not only by the Bloomsbury intellectuals of Rita Hinden's *Socialist Commentary*, but equally by Morgan Phillips' unduly neglected and controversial pamphlet of 1960, *Labour in the Sixties*, with its coded call for a 'forward-looking' (i.e. non-doctrinaire) policy. We were all revisionists now, it seemed – but with what precise range of programmes in view? Down to Gaitskell's unexpected death in early 1963, his party was still finding it difficult to articulate its faith in contemporary guise. There remained a powerful feeling that the essence of British socialism had already been enacted in the years 1945–51. The next phase of the onward march was hard to define.

The Wilson era

A new impetus came with the advent of Harold Wilson to the leadership in February 1963. His was still a powerful party, feared by its opponents. The records of the Tories during the Eden, Macmillan and Home era in 1955–64 confirm this to the full. These Tories were watchful, prudent custodians of Attlee's consensus. Wilson now added to this latent strength a zest for power. Old debates over the meaning and purpose of socialism were not resolved so much as by-passed. Wilson, a former civil servant apparatchik devoted to the corporate approach, had acquired a spurious reputation for left-wing views when he resigned with Bevan in 1951. But he was above all a centrist and an opportunist, and was thus an ideal reconciler. He made a virtue, among his dogmatic brethren, of averting his gaze from 'theology'. Instead of raising difficult questions about social equality or the location and character of economic power, Wilson chose to link socialism with modernisation, technical efficiency and industrial growth. Socialism, he declared at the 1963 annual party conference to the (apparently believing) delegates, was 'about science'. This appeal, skilfully tailored to the managers, skilled workers, professionals and other *déclassé* middle-class personnel loosely identified with the 'white heat' phase of later industrial growth, was highly effective for some time. It built on the sense of social fluidity noticed by a range of observers from Morgan Phillips to Mark Abrams in the early sixties. It also harnessed the idea of socialism, not to a disappearing industrial past, a Jerusalem of the Celtic twilight, but to the contemporary crucible of change. Tony Benn's published diaries, *Out of the Wilderness,* vividly convey the rare passion that this technocratic appeal could evoke in one intelligent young socialist. Nor should this science-based rhetoric be derided. In his time as leader of the opposition in 1963–4, Harold Wilson made perhaps the one and only attempt in Labour's 87-year history to relate the party's instincts to contemporary social change and future technical advance, to make nineteenth-century socialism become the cult of the new.

This strategy had much success amongst middle-class voters in the suburbs and dormitory constituencies, those who had turned rightwards from 1950 on. Under Wilson Labour gained a narrow electoral victory in 1964, and then a far more substantial triumph by almost one hundred seats in 1966. Labour staked its claim to modernity. Under Wilson, the party, triumphant in Oxford and Cambridge, cathedral cities like York, seaside resorts like Brighton, affluent suburbs like Hampstead and rural outposts like Cardiganshire, seemed genuinely to have found its second wind.

There have been some attempts since then to try to build up Wilson's ministries of 1964–70 into a paler version of 1945. It is true that the later sixties, years of high spending and active public enterprise with quangos galore, of permissive emancipation and social experiment, look to many a most attractive alternative to the philistine 'enterprise culture' of Thatcherite Britain now. But the comparison of 1964 with 1945 takes us hardly any distance at all. None of the preconditions of success, either in the structure of the party or its policies, was present a second time around. The outcome of the Wilson era was indeed to hasten the decline of the party and with more damaging results than anything the fifties had brought. While former participants in the Attlee government, a left-winger like Bevan no less than a right-winger like Gaitskell, could take genuine pride in that administration's achievement, the Wilson years brought merely divisiveness and disillusion. If the Attlee government spawned the still optimistic socialist critique of Aneurin Bevan, the Wilson ministries generated the despairing protest of Tony Benn which largely rejected every feature of the governments in which he served for eleven years.

One aspect of the Wilson period which proved especially damaging was evidence of Labour's sheer technical incompetence. A government which had come to power to modernise and to plan had no clear strategy on how to do so. The pre-election propaganda about science was not followed up, and the government's main scientific adviser, the eminent anatomist Sir Solly Zuckerman, became progressively disillusioned. The much-vaunted Ministry of Economic Affairs became a fiasco as the rival egos of George Brown and James Callaghan collided. The economy was never under proper control; an especially alarming sterling crisis in July 1966 was followed, far too late in the judgement of many economists, by devaluation late in 1967. The last two years of Labour's economic management were a time of severe retrenchment and general 'hard slog' under Jenkins. Again, the high and rising morale of party workers in the constituencies, so evident in the Attlee period, did not long survive the election of March 1966. From that time onwards, Labour's erosion in the country went on relentlessly, with party membership collapsing and party organisation unable or unwilling to combat Trotskyist or other entryism within disintegrating local parties. Constituency activists far removed from these extremes were deeply disillusioned by policies from a Labour government which implied a dilution of the Welfare State, a suspicious attitude to black immigrants, and servile endorsement of the American policy of mass bombing of the hapless peasants of South Vietnam. Each of these weakened popular support with no real compensation. On public expenditure cuts, racial policies and defence, the Tories, even under the unspectacular leadership of Heath, held most of the aces.

Worst of all, the relations of the party with the trade unions, the very lynch-pin of the triumphs of 1945–51, deteriorated beyond measure. There were repeated clashes between government and an increasingly left-led TUC over efforts to impose some kind of incomes policy. The Transport Workers' leader, Frank Cousins, left the Wilson government in protest. In 1969 Barbara Castle's Industrial Relations Bill (based on her White Paper 'In place of strife') led to a massive clash between Wilson and a handful of ministerial associates, and powerful TUC bosses like Jack Jones and Hugh Scanlon. In the end, deserted by most of his colleagues, and openly flaunted by Callaghan who challenged the Prime Minister to dismiss him, if he dared, Wilson had to climb down in humiliating circumstances. The unions, increasingly unpopular, now seemed overmighty and ungovernable. The axis between party and unions suddenly seemed frail indeed. The aftermath was a general fall in the government's credibility. Wilson's highly personal, covert style of operations, his intense obsession with the media and internal conspiracy, added to the erosion. The outcome was that, against all the odds it seemed, Labour was defeated in 1970 after a flat and complacent campaign marked by a falling turn-out (only 72 per cent) and notable apathy amongst Labour voters. The vaunted renewal of the Wilson years had proved to be a supreme, whimper-like illusion.

Changes since 1970

The years since 1970 have seen growing disintegration for much of the time. In the period of Tory government in 1970–74 Labour emerged as an uninspiring opposition, divided over Europe, devolution and defence, with a marked loss of support even in its old strongholds in Wales and Scotland. Wilson himself stayed on as leader and, to his apparent surprise, regained office on a minority basis in March 1974 in the aftermath of the miners' strike. In October of that year Labour slightly improved its position and gained the barest of overall majorities, but one still dependent on the Liberals. The years of Labour government in 1974–9 were not wholly barren. Wilson himself stayed on until April 1976. He had few initiatives to offer on any area of policy; not even alleged MI5 surveillance could unearth one. Promising novelties such as the National Enterprise Board came to little. But he did perform one supreme and characteristic service for his party, when he held it together over the Common Market issue by adopting the stratagem of a referendum. Labour emerged with no very clear policy on Europe, but at least the party still maintained a credible existence. Callaghan as Prime Minister from April 1976 was more effective in many ways, not least because of his calmer, less paranoid style of command. There was a desperate crisis over the national finances in 1976, leading to huge cuts in public expenditure at the behest of the International Monetary Fund. Callaghan handled his Cabinet with remarkable skill during this period. Thereafter the economy showed distinct signs of improvement under the aegis of Denis Healey, with production rising steadily, the pound stronger, inflation and unemployment both falling. There were many observers in 1978 who believed that, if the Prime Minister chose his timing with precision, Labour might yet scrape home for another term of office.

In fact, events largely beyond Callaghan's control were destroying the party from within. The immense cost inflation of the post-1973 years exacted its social and political toll. The unions, always Callaghan's trump card, continued to diverge from a rapport with the government after the flirtation with the so-called social contract up to mid-1976. Attempts by the government to impose some curb on wages as part of an anti-inflation package met with strong resistance. In the constituencies, the very inertia of the government's policies encouraged the traditional centrifugal forces within this most diffuse of parties. Under the powerful leadership of Tony Benn, the constituency parties managed to force through mandatory reselection of parliamentary candidates after Labour's defeat in the 1979 election, with new controls upon party policy and the leadership. Callaghan's last phase down to the end of 1980 saw open warfare between different sections in the movement. The formation of the Social Democrats in early 1981 saw the defection of major figures like Roy Jenkins, David Owen and Shirley Williams. Tension built up further during the unhappy leadership of Michael Foot thereafter, with a convulsive and damaging fight for the relatively unimportant post of deputy leader between Tony Benn and Denis Healey. A cataclysmic by-election defeat at Bermondsey in early 1982 was especially damaging. Beneath the surface, Foot's leadership in 1980–83 was, indeed, not without achievement. He managed to marginalise Benn and create the 'soft-left' majority which propelled Neil Kinnock into the leadership in 1983. But the general public saw only a party divided and at odds with itself. The breaking away of the Social Democrats in early 1981 confirmed this impression.

Throughout the seventies and early eighties, it was evident that Labour was changing its social composition. From being a broad alliance of the mass trade unions, along with select layers of the intelligentsia in the forties and fifties, it was now being taken over by a narrow range of interest groups. Instead of being headed by large unions composed mainly of manual workers, the party was increasingly influenced by public-sector and white-collar unions which had sprung up since 1960 – NUPE, COHSE, NALGO, ASTMS and others. They were often more sectional in their approach and more loosely led than unions in the past. In the Winter of Discontent in 1978–79 (launched, admittedly, by Ford car workers and oil-tanker lorry-drivers), it was public-sector unions who were identified with the closure of schools, the run-down of public services such as refuse collection and even the failure to dig graves. All these events rebounded heavily against the unions in 1979 and 1983. Another growing feature of the period was for local Labour parties to become less broad-based. Frequently they would be representative mainly of clients of Labour-led local authorities such as council housing-estate tenants. Again, these years were marked by local Labour parties, especially in several London boroughs, being captured by minority interest groups, perhaps feminist women, perhaps blacks, perhaps representatives of homosexuals or lesbians, perhaps the Irish – all single-issue pressure-groups of a peculiarly intense kind. In local government, this was popularly identified with the rise of the so-called 'loony left' phenomenon. Often these movements did reflect a genuine commitment by excluded or persecuted groups to making municipal socialism work; men like Ken Livingstone or David Blunkett could reflect the virtues as well as the demerits of this kind of movement on the GLC or in South Yorkshire. But the general public, regaled with accounts of harassment of 'racist' or 'sexist' schoolteachers or librarians, declarations of solidarity with the Nicaraguan Sandinista or the Mozambique Frelimo, or the establishment of gay workshops, was not encouraged to vote Labour. In this guise at least, permissiveness, a possible bonus for Labour in the sixties, was an incubus in the eighties.

All these internal developments helped to damage Labour. In the 1983 election, each was used devastatingly by a hostile press to show the party as doctrinaire, even revolutionary. The party's fall to only 209 seats from a peak of 394 in 1945, and only 27.6 per cent of the vote, its lowest share since 1918, was the result. Neil Kinnock, elected leader in October 1983, then tried to impose his leadership, with much initial success. He vigorously confronted Militant tendency and other left extremists, and put up a personally strong showing in the 1987 election. But the outcome was yet another heavy defeat by over one hundred seats, and renewed evidence of long-term decline. For the next eighteen months, Labour continued to lag far behind in the polls. Labour's main consolation was that at least the Alliance had been soundly thrashed as the putative alternative voice of opposition to Thatcherism. The collapse of the SDP after the polling, and the subsequent emergence of the Democrats from the ashes of the Alliance, encouraged Labour to believe that it still had a future at least as a party of opposition. The success of the 1920s in ditching the Liberals had been re-enacted. Indeed the Liberals had, nominally, ceased to exist. But the prospects of power and government seemed far off.

The problems for Labour

What the recent past has revealed is the existence of certain elements of weakness long dormant within the party. Evidence mounts of the rapid break-up of the historic, classic, cohesive, back-to-back working class. This had been the staple of Keir Hardie's constituency and, indeed, of Attlee's, years later. One cheerful school of thought maintains that Labour's years of greatness to 1951 also marked the climax of British football, and that both these proletarian interests declined in tandem thereafter. Perhaps symbolically, the one popular memory of the Wilson years is that England won the World Cup! But clearly, this decline in working-class cohesion (perhaps less evident in parts of Wales and Scotland if the 1987 election results are observed) has made it much more complicated for Labour to build up a natural majority. Coronation Street is almost as much of an historical exhibit as the age of chivalry by now.

Alongside this, the popularity and influence of the trade unions are far less notable today than in the post-1945 period. The Winter of Discontent was followed by restrictions imposed by the Thatcher government on the practices and privileges of trade unionism, amidst much popular approval and only muted Labour opposition. The 1987 general election saw the unions less directly implicated in the political process than in any previous election since Taff Vale at the turn of the century. Labour's alliance no longer obviously rested on a diminishing and somewhat discouraged trade union movement, even if men like Laird, Edmonds, Sawyer and Jordan suggested a new and refreshingly forward-looking leadership. Conversely, the devastating harm done to Labour's prospects (and, indeed, to his own miners' union) by the virtually apolitical ex-Communist Arthur Scargill beggars description. The expulsion of the electricians from the TUC in September 1988 suggested a further, damaging erosion. Some now questioned whether the old Labour/trade union alliance had a viable future.

Again, the idea of socialism no longer commands the support it once did. Indeed, despite the commendable ideological efforts of politicians like Hattersley and Gould and academics like Bernard Crick, there has been no major statement of socialist principle since Crosland's *Future of Socialism* appeared in 1956. The leftish intelligentsia, that famous 'thin red line' extending from Great

Turnstile via Bush House to Golders Green, has lost much of its *élan*. The Labour press (notably the *New Statesman*) lacked the cogency of the Kingsley Martin years when it acted as mentor to third-World nationalist leaders across the globe. The merger of the *New Statesman* with *New Society* in 1987 was a portent. The exotic, Euro-Communist designer appeal of *Marxism Today* (representing, after all, a party which wins less than 1 per cent of the vote) is hardly much compensation. On the far left, Benn-type socialism of the seventies looks a waning force (as Benn's heavy defeat by Kinnock in the 1988 leadership contest confirmed), while here, no less than on the centre-right, there are cries for revision, realism and a fresh start. Socialism, therefore, presents its problems for Labour now. So, too, does democracy. The Bennite upsurge of the seventies represented, in some quarters, a suppressed but genuine protest against the inert and unprincipled leadership of the Wilson era, a peasants' revolt against high politics and closet rule. But Labour's 'Glasnost', the delicate balance between grassroots vitality, always open to entryism, and a firm and respected leadership, remains an acute problem, even under the direction of Neil Kinnock. Prescott's strong challenge to Hattersley as deputy leader in 1988 provided vivid illustration of the point.

Finally, there is evidently much less enthusiasm now for the legitimacy of the state, the idea of central planning and bureaucratic control, the notion that the gentleman from Whitehall knows best. The consul-style mandarin has turned into the joke figure of *Yes Minister*. Old-style statism commanded natural support (or perhaps deferential acceptance) in the collectivist aftermath of a people's war after 1945. In the eighties, with home ownership, share ownership (until the autumn 1987 crash) and consumer affluence conspicuous (in southern and eastern England at least) Labour's centralist programme from the thirties, with its Fabian antecedents, no longer looks appealing or relevant. Meanwhile, the economic holocaust of the seventies has undermined the ethic of the Keynes-style managers and planners from within, and self-confidence has gone with it. In particular, the panacea of nationalisation or other forms of public ownership has lost its credibility. Morrisonian public-board enterprise was condemned by Labour in 1986 as 'monolithic' and 'bureaucratic'. The lurch towards privatisation by the Conservatives has not been very vigorously opposed by party or unions. Thus the very agency of Labour's economic approach has been removed, with efforts to concoct socialist investment or social market programmes vainly trying to fill the gap.

The future

It is far too early to pronounce a requiem for the Labour Party. After all, it was central to the making of postwar Britain. The Attlee concensus of 1945, the mixed economy, welfare democracy, full employment, social peace, governed the ethos of the nation down to 1979. Mrs Thatcher herself finds it hard to extricate herself from its coils. The current writing down of Labour's prospects should always be qualified by the astonishing anti-Labour bias in the daily press, and the well-known SDP/Democrat tendencies of fashionable reviewers in the weeklies and Sundays. Several old sources of internal controversy, such as the Common Market or the right of council tenants to purchase their homes, have been safely put to rest.

Nevertheless, it is beyond dispute that Labour needs to find a fresh kind of appeal, new levels of support, a different kind of strategy. The moral from the 1988 party conference seemed to be that Labour must direct itself towards the imperatives of decentralisation in decision making and the needs of the share-owning consumer and his or her family; but the intellectual guidelines for such an approach are so far lacking. There is, as yet, no successor to the intellectual output of the Labour Research Department under Michael Young or Peter Shore in earlier days. Defence policy is in a particular state of flux. At present, Labour looks like a frankly nostalgic party. Its appeal is too often to the past, to its own alternative past, the world of Tonypandy and the Jarrow march, of Clem and Nye and the legend of 1945. A movement committed to future change and a socialist transformation looks to the ages in heroic contemplation of past leaders and age-old triumphs, while the radicalism comes from the Thatcherite enemy.

But the party may yet dislodge itself from this cultural rut, and resume an onward movement. One (perhaps the only) moral for the historian is that life remains full of surprises. In the late eighties, the post-oil British economic base is insecure, the impetus, direction and future leadership of Thatcherism uncertain. The disarray in the balance of payments throughout 1988, followed by steep rises in interest rates and rising inflation fuelled by a credit explosion, offered Labour new political opportunities. The backlash against centralism may now turn against the poll-taxing, core-curricular Tories. Public opinion polls suggest that, on broad domestic issues like health, education and employment the mood remains 'Labourish', as in 1945, and may remain so*.

Key dates, 1945–1987

1945	May	Labour leaves Churchill's wartime coalition.
	July	Labour wins landslide general election victory with 394 seats; Attlee becomes Prime Minister.
1947	Feb.	Winter fuel crisis.
	Nov.	Cripps becomes Chancellor and begins austerity programme.
1950	Feb.	General election: Labour, with 315 seats, narrowly re-elected.
1951	Apr.	Resignation of Bevan and Wilson from Attlee government.
	Oct.	Labour, with 295 seats, defeated by the Conservatives.
1955	May	General election: Labour, with 277 seats, defeated again.
	Dec.	Gaitskell succeeds Attlee as party leader.
1956	Feb.	Bevan re-enters Shadow Cabinet. Crosland's *Future of Socialism* appears.
1959	Oct.	General election: Labour, with 258 seats, defeated a third time.
1960	Oct.	Gaitskell defeated at Scarborough party conference over nuclear weapons.
1963	Feb.	After Gaitskell's death, Wilson becomes party leader.
1964	Oct.	General election: Labour, with 317 seats, wins narrow majority and Wilson becomes Prime Minister.
1966	Mar.	General election: Labour, with 364 seats, wins majority of nearly 100 and Wilson remains in office.
1969	July	Clash between Wilson government and TUC over bill to implement *In Place of Strife*.
1970	June	General election: Labour, with 288 seats, defeated by the Conservatives.
1974	Feb.	General election: Labour, with 301 seats, forms a minority administration under Wilson.
	Oct.	Second general election: Labour retains office with 319 seats.
1976	Apr.	Callaghan succeeds Wilson as party leader and Prime Minister.

1978–9		'Winter of Discontent' among the unions over wage demands.
1979	June	General election: Labour, with 269 seats, defeated by the Conservatives.
1980	Nov.	Foot succeeds Callaghan as Labour leader.
1981	Oct.	Healey narrowly defeats Benn in deputy leadership contest.
1983	May	General election: Labour with 209 seats, again defeated.
	Oct.	Kinnock succeeds Foot as party leader.
1987	June	General election: Labour, with 229 seats, defeated a third time.
1988	Oct.	Kinnock easily defeats Benn in leadership contest; Hattersley defeats Prescott for deputy leadership.
1989	June	Labour wins Euro-elections with 45 seats to Tories' 31.

---

* Since the above article was completed in late 1988, Labour has greatly improved its standing in the opinion polls to lead (August 1989) by 9–10 per cent. It also performed strongly in by-elections and the European elections. However, these gains appeared to result from errors by the Thatcher government, both over presentation (e.g. the re-shuffle of July 1989) and over economic, health and environmental policies. They are entirely compatible, in my view, with the long-term diagnosis of Labour's problems offered above.

2

The Conservative Party Since 1945

JOHN RAMSDEN

The Conservative Party is customarily presented in the eighties as a party that has turned its back on much of its earlier policies, style and character. The departure of Norman Tebbitt from the party chairmanship in 1987, the retirement from active politics of William Whitelaw which followed shortly afterwards, and Margaret Thatcher's becoming the longest-serving modern Prime Minister in 1989, all provided political columnists with occasions for timely reflections on what has changed. So, for example, Woodrow Wyatt wrote in *The Times* of:

> the transformation of the Tory Party. Its natural leaders were once gentlemen, well connected politically and socially, and, as the Liberal Party disappeared, strengthened by gentlemen of Whiggish paternalist tendencies. Such people believed that those like themselves sitting comfortably at the top had a duty to look after those at the bottom, as officers took care of their troops and landed proprietors of their tenants. As their personal fortunes dwindled they saw the state as the alternative provider of this benevolence. So the welfare state was accepted, and the Conservative Party became almost an alternative Labour Party, but with the 'right' people running it. Mrs Thatcher instinctively saw that this meant terminal decline for the country, which was becoming stifled and bereft of independent initiative by cramping Socialism, whichever party was in power. So, where are the gentlemen now? Hardly any are in the Cabinet, and those who are have been converted to her

18

belief that self-help is better than state help. The old Tory leaders tried to identify with ordinary people, but were too distant from them accurately to understand their aspirations. Mrs Thatcher is one of them and understands them perfectly, thus making the Tory Party a One Nation party in a sense it never was before.

This bold statement encompasses many themes common to other commentators – the 'semi-socialism' of Conservatism before Thatcher, the social revolution of the *Upwardly Mobile* (as Tebbitt's autobiography of 1988 entitles it), the assumption that this modern Conservatism is somehow based on 'ordinary' people in a way that Macmillan's brand of politics was not; above all the personalisation of the change around Thatcher and her instincts. The analysis could be mirrored in a large number of such articles, notably those by Brian Walden and Bernard Levin; it is no accident that Wyatt, Walden, Levin and others who see the change so starkly were themselves converts to the right during Thatcher's time – more royalist than the Queen? But the analysis can be found also on the left; John Mortimer, no admirer of Margaret Thatcher, created in *Paradise Postponed* the character of Leslie Titmus, a paradigm for the 'upwardly mobile' in modern Toryism.

There are however flaws in this entire approach. The chronological profile of British Conservatism since the Second World War is, to say the least, susceptible to other explanations. In *Ruling Performance* (ed. Hennessy and Seldon, Blackwell, 1987), Lord Fraser of Kilmorack described the same period as a slow tactical retreat by the party before the advance of socialism, only for the Conservatives to set to work on rolling back socialism and the socialist state when the opportunity arose after 1970. The same view can be put in less overtly political ways: the period since 1945 can be seen as a time in which Conservatives, in order to survive as a governing party, had to accept ideas about economics and welfare policy which derived mainly from such Liberals as Keynes and Beveridge, but then struck back towards goals with which they were more sympathetic when the fallacies of the liberal consensus were exposed by the passage of time. All such scenarios assume a foresight and a flexibility in tactical manoeuvre which is unlikely even in the most pragmatic of parties. But they also point to ways in which Conservatism in the eighties seems to have more in common with its prewar ancestor than with the intervening generations. Any government which battened down the hatches in the face of an international economic blizzard that created mass unemployment, offering only the argument that 'There is no alternative' as solace to the unemployed, is bound to evoke parallels with the National Government of the thirties. Retrenchment, attempts to secure balanced budgets in the pursuit of 'sound money', and a pursuit of the rapid extension of home-ownership are further parallels. The mistaken belief of opposition parties that Conservatives could not be re-elected in such economic circumstances offers another comparison, though in both decades it was the divisions of the opposition that help to explain how that came about in any case. Before 1939, as after 1979, the Conservative leadership was seen by opponents as dictatorial and wilful, given to media manipulation and unfair recourse to the courts to sustain itself; no Conservative leader since Neville Chamberlain has been as widely and bitterly hated by opponents as Thatcher – and there is little doubt that Chamberlain would thoroughly approve of what Conservatism in the eighties has been about, or that he would have had misgivings about the earlier period. It should be added that no Conservative leader since Churchill has been so much admired by party supporters as Thatcher. No doubt both the hatred and the admiration would be taken by the Prime Minister's entourage as signs of how much she has achieved.

The same sense in which the immediate postwar years now seem to be an interruption to the normal current of Conservative history emerges from the social character of the leadership. In 1911, the party chose as leader Andrew Bonar Law, who could hardly have been further from the aristocratic, 'Hotel Cecil' character of late-Victorian Conservatism, a self-made member of the unpolished bourgeoisie. Austen Chamberlain, Stanley Baldwin and Neville Chamberlain, who led the party from 1921 to 1940, all reflected industrial, provincial, upper middle class Conservatism – if with more polish and education than Law. After thirty years, the election of Churchill in 1940 opened a new phase – with Macmillan related by marriage to the Devonshires (despite protestations about his Scottish crofter background), Churchill a scion of the Marlboroughs, Eden from an old gentry family, and Home actually a land-owning aristocrat himself. For a quarter of a century then, Conservative leaders were all from upper class families, quite different from the generations before or after. The succession of Heath and Thatcher from 1965, representing the managerial, suburban middle class rather than owners of industry (as industry itself had largely changed over from family proprietors) makes more sense as a further progression from the Baldwin dynasty than from that of Macmillan; the abrupt resumption of that progression after interruption may indeed explain the audible grinding of gears that accompanied the modernisation of Conservative policy in 1965. So far the common assumption of social change at the heart of political change seems persuasive, but the argument needs to be set against important continuities before any conclusions can be drawn.

Pre and postwar continuities

The most obvious and important continuity is the fact that the Conservatives have remained a generally successful party. By the end of the 1987 Parliament, the Conservatives will have governed for about 29 of the 46 years since the war, all the time in single-party government and with an effective working majority. This is in itself not new: in the century since the 1886 Irish crisis effectively re-balanced British politics, the party has also governed for about two-thirds of the time. The near despair of 1945 and the acute party crises of 1965 and 1975 must both be set against this record of success – and expectation of success.

The Conservatives have always enjoyed an organisational lead over other parties, not apparent in 1945 but certainly re-established by 1950 and ever-present since. By any measurement, such as the number of members and activists, the number of party employees, the amount of money available for electioneering, that lead has been continuous. Much of the advantage doubtless accrued to the party simply as the best defender of industry and property, but much too is owed to a readiness to innovate. In this field the Conservatives have been the least *conservative* of all British parties: the poster campaigns run by Colman, Prentis and Varley in 1958–9, use of opinion polls and panel surveys in the sixties, and co-ordinated down-market campaigning through Saatchi and Saatchi in 1978–9 are all examples of Conservative experiments that other parties had to follow. Difficulties like the poor quality of television broadcasts in 1959 or the mid-campaign crisis of 1987 only indicate the height of expectations: Conservatives expected to dominate the campaigning as well as to win the vote.

What is less obvious is how far the Conservatives have remained a *unionist* party in the context of the United Kingdom. For most of the period since 1945 this was shown clearly enough by the solid phalanx of Ulster Unionist MPs who took the Conservative whip. It was indeed the loss of that support after the abolition of the Stormont Parliament in 1972 that cost the party office, for with the traditional Unionist backing, Heath could have retained power in 1974. Conservatives in many parts of Scotland continued to call themselves Unionists, and the strength of that identity was shown when the party was alone in campaigning for a 'No' vote in the 1979 devolution referendum. The same reflex was shown when the party's Central Council overwhelmingly threw out a platform recommendation (in itself rather a rarity) to drop the word 'Unionist' from the official party name. It was in the perpetuation of the loyalties and instincts of unionism that Conservatism remained strong in such places as Liverpool and Glasgow, and it is no accident that no alternative basis for Conservative strength was found when religion and nationality ceased to be dominant issues in such places in the sixties.

With these exceptions though, the regional basis of party strength has remained remarkably constant. Conservatives have consistently done better in the southeastern half of England, suburban constituencies and rural areas, than in Wales and Scotland, northern England or inner cities. The distribution of seats in 1983 roughly matched that of 1935, when the Conservatives and Labour won a similar share of the seats. What *did* change though was the number of seats in the party's southeastern stronghold region, as economic development tilted the balance of population. Now that half of the population of Britain live to the south of Birmingham, it is a greater political benefit to have strong party roots there. The southeastern counties and London suburbs, always the best Conservative area since the days of Peel and Disraeli, had 165 MPs in 1935 but 235 MPs by 1983 – an increase of over 40 per cent. It is no wonder that the party of 'Selsdon man' – and indeed of 'Finchley woman' – has prospered.

A final element of continuity may seem to be more apparent in the eighties than in the fifties, the readiness of the party to receive converts from other beliefs. Baldwin once remarked that Conservatism must constantly recruit from the left and the young, and it was indeed the accretion of Liberal Unionists after 1886, and of National Liberals and Liberal Nationals after the interwar coalitions that helped to top up Conservative strength. The postwar creation of the Young Conservative organisation was an attempt to 'recruit the young', as were later experiments with cinema advertising and pop concerts. But recruitment from the left was more problematic after 1945, as the Labour Party showed a far greater reluctance to split than Liberals of earlier periods. Churchill's offer of office to Liberal Leader Clement Davies in 1951 was undoubtedly an attempt to absorb what was left of the Liberals, but a temptation that Davies rejected. All the same, even while Labour was relatively cohesive in the twenty years after 1945, three Labour backbenchers who crossed the floor of the Commons were welcomed and given the Tory whip, and three former Labour MPs and one former Liberal were later elected as Conservatives after a time outside the House. The reception of Reg Prentice when he crossed the floor in 1977 was also a warm one, with a safe Conservative seat and ministerial office coming his way. The number of equivalent moves from right to left was not comparable, but neither was their reception: Humphry Berkeley was accepted by Labour but went on only to be Labour candidate in a safe Conservative seat and inevitable defeat. It is no doubt easier for a pragmatic, conservative grouping to welcome converts than for an ideological party of the left, but the period since 1945 has shown none the less that the Conservatives remain extremely open to converts. In any case, the few converts at national level need to be placed alongside the steadier trickle in local councils – for example in Walsall or in Oxford, where former Labour councillors bolstered Tory strength – and by the increasing influx of intellectuals to the Thatcher colours: Max Beloff, Hugh Thomas and Paul Johnson are just a few of those who found a ready welcome at the highest level – others include John Wain, Kingsley Amis and Tom Stoppard.

Social class base

All theories about social change in the Conservative Party are difficult to reconcile with the evidence. If the education and occupations of elected and defeated candidates are analysed, there

Table 2.1

	1951	1959	1970	1983
The background of Conservative MPs (percentage of total)				
Occupation				
Professional	41	46	45	45
Business	37	30	30	36
Miscellaneous				
white collar	22	23	24	19
Manual	0	1	1	1
Education				
Public school	75	72	74	70
Of which:				
Eton/Harrow/Winchester	33	29	25	16
The background of defeated Conservative candidates (percentage of total)				
Occupation				
Professional	44	40	48	42
Business	33	40	37	36
Miscellaneous				
white collar	16	15	13	17
Manual	5	5	1	5
Education				
Public school	42	30	41	40

appears to be virtually no change anyway (see Table 2.1). For the whole of this century, about three-quarters of Tory MPs have been educated at public schools, while defeated candidates in less good constituencies have also had less privileged backgrounds. In occupation, it is difficult to see much change since 1945 or any real difference between winners and losers. But caution is needed in applying such findings, not least because the basis of comparison is itself changing over time. As the proportion of boys going to public schools doubled in the thirty years after 1950, so the steady proportion of Conservative MPs from independent schools has actually come from a wider cross-section of the public. This is borne out by the one clear trend, the steady decline in numbers coming from the most elite schools of all: Eton, Harrow and Winchester. These had provided nearly half of all Tory MPs at the start of the century, were down to a third in 1951, a quarter in 1970 and less than a sixth in the eighties. Even this clear trend is difficult to relate to the highest political level, partly because a seat in Cabinet owes as much to luck, ability and the whim of Prime Ministers as to the party's character. So Macmillan's

Cabinets were the most socially exclusive of any since the war, but they also represent the high point of Keynesian management economics and the pursuit of national consensus by Conservatives. It is tempting to conclude with Woodrow Wyatt that such paternalist traditions vanished with Macmillan's generation of leaders, but once again the facts will not bear out the theories. Thatcher's Cabinet in 1983, by which time she had her own choice of colleagues rather than a team largely evolved by her predecessor, closely resembled the parliamentary party in its social character. Fifteen out of twenty-one Cabinet ministers had been to public schools and there was no obvious correlation between background and policy orientation: the keenest Thatcherites were Joseph (Harrow) and Howe (Winchester), while the six who had not been to public school included not only Tebbitt and Parkinson of the 'dries' but also Walker and Biffen of the 'wets'. Subsequent promotions and dismissals have not changed the pattern.

The broad character of the party is not really very different to the one that Jean Blondel analysed thirty years ago. In its social character there is still a pyramid: Conservative voters were not a cross-section of the electorate, but did contain large numbers of people from every class; members were a degree more exclusive, with a heavier middle class orientation, and constituency activists and local councillors much more so; MPs and national party officers continued to come from a narrow social group. Twenty years ago, it was already clear to political scientists that there were a multiplicity of reasons that persuaded many working class voters to back Conservative candidates, but two broad motivations dominated; one was for reasons of habit and deference for those who identified more with nation than with class, and the other through a pragmatic calculation of self interest among those whose point of identity was individual or family. As the Conservative leadership has become more middle class, the balance may well have swung more to the second of these explanations (with a resulting need for economic success to underpin support, even more than before) but Thatcher's stout articulation of nationality and the 'national interest' against the EEC, Argentina, non-white immigrants and militant trade unions has indicated a constant awareness of the value of the deference vote. Overall though, the social composition of the Conservative vote in the eighties is not very different from that of the sixties.

One warning needs to be added. In any party of the right change comes only slowly, especially if that party remains relatively successful, but it takes in any case a generation for social changes to emerge clearly. The Maxwell-Fyfe reforms of 1949 certainly helped a slightly wider cross-section of classes to get into the House, but it was not until the sixties that those men reached the top. If Thatcher's leadership really is initiating a major social change in the party, it will not be fully measurable until the end of the century.

Years of recovery, 1945–1957

The overwhelming election defeat of 1945 came as a terrible shock to a party which had dominated Britain since 1918, and not least for Churchill who had not foreseen it. He was fortunate, however, in being the only modern Conservative to lead the party to a shattering defeat and survive as leader. The party, unlike the nation, was simply too grateful to Churchill for war services to ditch him, even if sometimes seething under his fitful lead in opposition and his increasing age. But his presence provided a valuable umbrella under which a real review of policy could take place. His own deliberate destruction in the war years of the collective Conservative leadership that he found in possession in 1940 had in any case removed most alternatives, and he completed the job by wrecking his predecessors' reputations once and for all in the first volume of his *War Memoirs*. The main task then was the re-creation of a Conservative identity and of confidence, both severely mauled by coalition and defeat in 1945. The opposition years were thus a time of internal re-building. Central Office and the Research Department were fully operational again by 1947; the drive for new members was spectacularly successful and reached three million in 1951, with the Young Conservatives being one of the fastest areas of growth. Membership then levelled off and went into a slow but steady decline; it had probably halved by 1970 and then fell a little further.

Mass membership was in itself a morale-booster, but it was also an opportunity for fund-raising and for widening participation. The Maxwell-Fyfe reforms not only outlawed the purchase of safe seats with candidates' contributions but also laid down that local parties must pay to central funds a fee appropriate to the party's local strength. The Conservative Political Centre sought both to put across party policies and to involve members in a two-way flow of ideas between leaders and the grassroots. The same commitment to the exchange of views came with the policy review, the Industrial Policy Committee of 1946–7, whose members toured the country taking evidence. The *Industrial Charter* which emerged was an unexciting document, more a set of principles than a manifesto, and mostly principles already in the 1945 manifesto. But in 1945, partly through folk memories of the thirties and the mood of sharing occasioned by the war, partly by Churchill's buccaneering campaign, the party's stance was obscured, and the public were not convinced that Conservatives really would support welfare reforms, a mixed economy and full employment. The *Industrial Charter* attempted the difficult task of convincing the public that the party meant what it had said in 1945, while convincing the party activists that it said something new. In this it was a great success precisely by avoiding too much detail.

The policy work also brought a new generation to the fore – R. A. Butler as chairman of the Research Department, Macmillan as a key member of the Industrial Policy Committee and Reginald Maudling as its secretary, Iain Macleod and Enoch Powell as policy workers with a hand in every document, Quintin Hogg as an expert draftsman brought in to advise on one key document and to write an elegant book-length *Case for Conservatism*. The prominence of all these men in the next twenty years and more owed something to reputations made or enhanced between 1945 and 1951. It is difficult, though, to show that all the work in opposition, cheering though it was for the activists, did much to win back power – except in the sense of eradicating once and for all the impression given in 1945 that Conservatives did not mean what they said. The return to power owed at least as much to the natural arousing of opposition to a Labour Party bent on major reforms and to the public's increasing irritation at austerity and restrictions continuing long into peacetime.

Two new issues arose almost accidentally, in response to the public mood. As Labour began to reduce controls, public demand ran ahead of what the government could easily do (especially while at war in Korea) and this opened up the way for the Conservatives to campaign to 'set the people free', a message that had more in common with Churchill's anti-socialist campaigning of 1945 than with the message of interdependence and partnership highlighted in policy work since. The pledge to build 300,000 houses a year, given at the 1950 party conference in response to members' wishes, was another large shift towards individualism and away from the state. Here though, the rhetoric needed to win an election and the detailed policy work came together. It was careful preparation before taking office that paved the way for Macmillan to redeem the pledge successfully in 1954. The period of opposition with its 'impressionist' policy-making (as Butler termed it) therefore left the party committed to the maintenance of the broad consensus on which the 1945 election had been fought, but also to the widening of choice and freedom which headed the public's own agenda by 1951. Within the party individual candidates gave greater emphasis to these different strands.

In terms of confidence 1945 took a long time to forget. By-election disappointments in 1949 led to recriminations, and even election victory in 1951 did not appear to have turned back the 1945 clock. It is not therefore at all surprising that Churchill's 1951 government proceeded with caution, accentuating continuity rather than change. The National Health Service was not greatly affected by the change of government, though the Conservatives did gradually push up the charges made for services after Labour had introduced the principle. The methods of economic policy also moved along existing pathways, hence the coining of the word 'Butskellism' to describe a consensus of policy. Token acts of denationalisation for steel and for road haulage in 1953 did not signal the closing down of the public sector, and new areas of competition in broadcasting and in new-town public houses were really only symbols of party differentiation. It was indeed tactically more advantageous to leave the great energy monopolies in public hands, both because that meant that their losses were a disguised subsidy from the taxpayer to the rest of industry (e.g. in the form of cheaper coal and electricity), but also so that the regular reported losses of railways and coal could serve as an argument against further nationalisation.

The few suggestions that Conservatives should promote share-ownership to widen the ownership of industry fell on deaf ears until the unit trust movement began to proselytise for the cause in the sixties. The public demand for freedom and ownership could be met more simply through houses and their contents. The housing boom of the fifties added two million to the national stock of dwellings, though half of this was in the public sector. Income tax reductions in 1953 and 1955 – five per cent off the standard rate overall – helped middle class purchasing power. Together with rapid advances in hire purchase this fuelled a consumer boom with the emphasis on cars (up 140 per cent in the decade), telephones (up 50 per cent), and consumer durable goods like washing machines, furniture and televisions. With the widening of affluence well under way the party's re-election in 1955 requires little explanation, particularly with a new and popular Prime Minister in Anthony Eden.

Eden, Macmillan and Home, 1955–1965

Party confidence was assisted by a symbolic by-election triumph in Sunderland in 1953 but particularly by the increased majority of 1955 and the advent with Eden of a postwar generation: Butler claimed that 1955 had 'destroyed for ever the myth that 1945 represented the beginning of some irreversible revolution'. Such bright hopes were rapidly dispelled, first by economic difficulties and then by the Suez crisis. The collapse of Eden's health at the end of 1956 opened the way for Macmillan, 'first in and first out over Suez', to become Prime Minister, but with an implicit mandate not to apologise for recent events. The Macmillan government reorientated Britain's colonial and defence policies, repaired relations with America, and in due course tried to follow the change of policy through by joining the Common Market. However, the entire operation had to be carried through behind a smokescreen of rhetoric which denied that much of substance was changing or needed to be changed.

In these taxing circumstances the Macmillan government mainly pursued the more popular parts of its domestic inheritance. The end of conscription could be seen as the biggest of all freedoms restored, but other policies with the same aims had bigger costs attached. The political need to regenerate the economy in 1958 led to the resignation of the Treasury ministers, worried by the inflationary impact of government expenditure. Macmillan's conviction that 'a little inflation does no harm' was clearly influenced by memories of interwar Stockton and the belief that much more harm would be done by deflation. Further tax cuts unleashed another boom which carried the government to a larger majority in 1959 and a peak of popularity in 1960. The price was paid in the 1961 recession, worse than that of 1956–7, and more resented because of the expectations of continuing growth which the government had itself aroused.

The last three years of Conservative government were beset by outside problems like espionage scandals, Rhodesia, and the failure to get into the EEC, which progressively damaged the Conservatives' reputation for competence and led to increasing criticism of Macmillan's laid-back 'Edwardian' style. More and more hung on the restoration of international economic competitiveness as the basis for growth and re-election. Hence experiments with indicative or informal planning from 1961, as in the creation of the National Economic Development Council, though these all involved a corporatist extension of state management which hardly accorded with setting people free. Macmillan's Cabinet purge of 1962 attempted to put a fresh and younger face to his team, but the strategy was pulled apart by his own retirement on health grounds in 1963, by the open fight for the leadership which followed, and by the refusal of Macleod and Powell to serve under the new leader, Home. Determined action in the Home government's one year, for example Heath's battle to end retail price-fixing, did something to show that the party had not run out of steam or ideas, and a consumer boom in 1963–4 very nearly generated enough popularity to win another election. It is tempting to speculate whether a Conservative win in 1964 – by no means unlikely if there had been no split in 1963 – would have led to further attempts to combine a dash for economic growth with a consensual, corporatist style. By that stage though, voices were already being raised against partnership with trade unionists, and were advocating different solutions. Defeat in 1964, if only by a whisker, brought them to far greater prominence.

The Heath experiment, 1965–1975

Within nine months of losing office, the Conservatives had a new leader who was seen as representing a different social constituency, a system for electing leaders for the first time, and a policy statement that abandoned many concepts pursued in government. *Putting Britain Right Ahead* committed Britain clearly to a European future, as Macmillan had not quite brought himself to do, and the refusal to oppose Labour's policy of sanctions against the illegal white Rhodesian government demonstrated an equally definite turn against the colonial past. Nonetheless, there were other areas where the sharpness of change was more apparent than real, the most serious of which was the promise to reform trade union law. It had remained an implicit concession to the need for national consensus right through from 1951 that the Conservatives would not provoke a fight over industrial relations, much as Baldwin had sought to avoid one in 1925: the appointment of the emollient Walter Monckton as Minister of Labour by Churchill seemed a promise of good intentions, and the involvement of the unions in the NEDC was an even clearer invitation to partnership. Tories had certainly made political capital out of wildcat strikes and demarcation disputes to embarrass Labour, but Conservative ministers had not proposed solutions. Now the unions became favourite scapegoats for economic decline, though by no means the only ones, for the new approach heralded a tougher stance towards industry too. The opposition period between 1964 and 1970 therefore marked a shift to more uncompromising policies long demanded by activists and backbenchers – the party's Industrial Relations Committee and the Society of Conservative Lawyers had both demanded trade union reform – but previously resisted by Prime Ministers because of their divisiveness and probable unpopularity. Rhetorically the party turned away from the idea that partnership would deliver prosperity and towards the view that the government should impose the tough action needed for growth. In response to Wilson's pragmatic Labour government, the promise of a tougher attitude could in itself generate popularity; it was certainly wildly popular with the Conservative rank and file, who now heard their leaders demanding things that they had wanted for years – less intervention, restrictions on the unions and lower taxes.

What was less clear was the political basis behind the rhetoric. As a leader elected in opposition Heath lacked the authority and patronage of Prime Minister and had to work with close colleagues who were in any case not at all keen to throw overboard all the experience of 1951–64. So trade union proposals were modified to allow for internal dissent, and the shadow Cabinet hardly even discussed the issue of incomes policy, for the probable disagreements were too painful to rake over. As a result, the most thorough policy review that any party has ever conducted papered over inner doubts about essentials, doubt even among those who would have to implement the policies. Major economic reforms would always be difficult without at least the option of intervention to mitigate short-term effects, but no such fail-back plans seem to have been made, no consideration of what level of unemployment (if any) would be an acceptable price to pay. Nor did the framers of industrial relations laws ever face up to the question of non-compliance; it was always cosily assumed that the unions would respect an electoral mandate.

As a result, the new rhetoric had by 1970 raised expectations among activists and voters, but the policy package had not been tested against enough 'what if . . .?' questions. That weakness was compounded when the Heath government encountered entirely unpredictable difficulties, the downturn in the world economy, the 1973 oil crisis, the swing of important trade unions to the left, and a spiral of violence in Ulster. By 1972 ministers were clearly not prepared to accept the unmitigated effects of their policies; the 'U-turn' of 1972 was thus a recalculation of timing and method, not a change of objectives, but since the new methods ran counter to earlier rhetoric, the party response was sharply critical. The recognition that the Industrial Relations Act was a dead letter, the adoption of unprecedented intervention in industry, and state regulation of prices and incomes all looked more like strategic defeats than a tactical withdrawal. When a political defeat by the miners was added in 1974 the party mood became distinctly mutinous. It is after all one thing to withstand demands for a policy, but quite different to offer that policy and then pull back. When the loss of power followed too, Heath's position was untenable.

New directions since 1975

In opposition between 1974 and 1979 there was an even clearer breach with the past. The speeches made by Sir Keith Joseph in

1974–5, published as *Reversing the Trend*, provided the most complete rejection of policies that all postwar governments had pursued. The Centre for Policy Studies which he formed with Margaret Thatcher in 1974 provided a pressure group for such free market ideas, but a younger generation of Conservative MPs had already been influenced by the books of Hayek and Friedman, by the quiet propagandising of the Mont Pelerin Society and the Institute of Economic Affairs, and by the speeches of Powell. Powell had scandalised front-benchers by calling for income tax at 4s 3d (or 21p in the pound) twenty years before Nigel Lawson as Chancellor made that his objective. But in rejecting what governments had done since 1945, there was no rejection of what Conservatives had said in 1970, or of the policies with which the Heath government had started. In that sense the Thatcher policies flowed quite naturally from the policy review of 1965, and from the lessons learned from Heath's attempt to put the new ideas into practice. As Patrick Jenkin said in 1988, 'Mrs Thatcher has achieved what Heath aspired to and could not achieve'.

Much of the character of the Conservative Party at any one time is derived from its leader, who sets the tone and much of the acceptable agenda. Nobody would now underestimate that fact in Margaret Thatcher's case. It is though still easy to underestimate how far she is a product of the party's shift of direction as well as the fuel in the machine. After 1974 it was clear that the party desperately wanted office and would not forgive a leader who did not win, but it was unusual in wanting quite specific policy objectives to be pursued too, many of them without regard for the consequences. After a decade in government in which Thatcher has largely delivered the goods to her supporters, it would be even more difficult for any successor to close the Pandora's Box of expectations that began to open in 1965 and crashed ajar in 1979. Any future Conservative leader will have to live not only with what Thatcher has done, but also with the expectations which her successes have raised among Conservatives. In this – as in so much else – she will be a difficult act to follow.

Key dates

1945 May   Churchill forms caretaker, mainly Conservative, government.
      July   General Election; big Labour win and worst Conservative showing since 1906.

1946	July	Lord Woolton becomes party chairman (to 1955).
1947	Oct.	Party conference approves the *Industrial Charter*.
1949	Oct.	*Maxwell Fyfe Report on Party Organisation* adopted.
1950	Feb.	General Election; narrow Labour win.
	Oct.	Party conference extracts pledge on housing from platform.
1951	Oct.	General Election; Churchill becomes Prime Minister with majority of 17.
1955	Apr.	Eden replaces Churchill as Prime Minister.
	May	General Election increases Conservative majority to 58.
1956	June	Tonbridge by-election demonstrates government unpopularity.
	Nov.	Suez Crisis; Nutting and Boyle resign.
1957	Jan.	Macmillan replaces Eden as Prime Minister.
1958	Jan.	Thorneycroft resigns with Treasury ministers over public spending.
1959	Oct.	General Election increases Conservative majority to 100.
1960	Feb.	Macmillan's 'Winds of Change' speech in South Africa.
1961	July	Lloyd's Pay Pause and establishment of NEDC.
1962	Mar.	Orpington by-election; Liberal gain of safe Conservative seat.
	July	'Night of the long knives': Macmillan sacks Lloyd and six other Cabinet ministers.
1963	June	Resignation of Profumo from War Office.
	Oct.	Home replaces Macmillan as Prime Minister; Macleod and Powell refuse to serve under Home.
1964	Oct.	General Election makes Wilson Prime Minister with majority of five.
1965	July	Heath defeats Maudling in first leadership election following Home's resignation. Party publishes *Putting Britain Right Ahead*.
1966	Mar.	General Election; Labour majority rises to 96.
1967	Apr.	Powell's 'Rivers of Blood' speech and dismissal from Shadow Cabinet.
1970	June	Unexpected Conservative General Election win; Heath becomes Prime Minister with majority of 30.
1972	Mar.	Industry Bill marks 'U-turn' on economic policy.
		Suspension of Stormont brings end of Conservative alliance with Ulster Unionists.
1974	Feb.	Labour minority government after miners' strike and General Election.
	Oct.	General Election returns Labour with small majority.
		Formation of Centre for Policy Studies.
1975	Feb.	Thatcher defeats Heath and then Whitelaw in leadership votes.
	July	Joseph publishes *Reversing the Trend*.
1976	Oct.	*The Right Approach* demonstrates onset of 'Thatcherism' in economic policy.
1979	May	General Election returns Thatcher as Prime Minister with majority of 43.

1982	Apr.	Argentina invades the Falklands, creation of War Cabinet.
1983	June	General Election increases Conservative majority to 146.
1984	Mar.	Beginning of year-long miners' strike.
1986	Apr.	Abolition of GLC and Metropolitan Counties.
1987	June	General Election; Conservative majority of 102.
1989	Jan.	Thatcher becomes longest-serving Prime Minister of the century.

3

The Liberal Party Since 1945

JOHN STEVENSON

Since the general election of 1987 third party politics in Britain have been in a state of flux, of which the long-term outcome is still unclear. Some commentators predict a permanently more confused and fragmented political scene with the Social and Liberal Democrats, Dr Owen's 'continuing SDP', discontented Liberals, as well as other minority groupings, such as Greens and Nationalists, competing for votes between the two major parties. Others see a future which might be described as 'two-and-a-half party politics' in which a chronically weaker third force, most probably the Social and Liberal Democrats, remains capable of having an impact on the shape of politics at the margins, but is still unable to compete for power at national level on equal terms. Others still continue to speculate whether a revitalised third force, under new leadership, might be capable of supplanting one of the other major parties and changing the face of British politics.

But for much of the period since 1945, the fortunes of third party politics, represented by the Liberal Party, offered no such prospects, indeed in the years after the Second World War it looked for a time as though the Liberal Party was doomed to extinction as a credible political force – a party with a great future behind it and no obvious hope of better things to come. Only slowly was it to revive, eventually reaching its more secure, but still uncertain, place in recent years. Probably the most useful way of looking at the evolution of the Liberal Party in the years since 1945 is to consider it as comprising three main phases: the period up to 1958 when its decline apparently continued the trends of the interwar years; the period from 1958 to 1981 when the party's fortunes began to revive under the stimulus of a series of spectacular by-election triumphs and more effective leadership; and the period since 1981 when the formation of the SDP and its Alliance with the Liberals brought the Liberal Party to its highest level of popular support and parliamentary success for decades.

The threat of extinction

The story of the Liberal Party between the wars was one of almost uninterrupted decline. Although a section of the party under Lloyd George was in coalition government with the Conservatives from the general election of 1918, Lloyd George's assumption of the premiership had split the party with the followers of the ex-Premier Asquith and the new Premier Lloyd George, each being organised with separate sets of whips. In the 1918 election, the once powerful Liberal Party fought as two separate entities: the Lloyd George or 'Coalition' Liberals and the Asquithian Liberals. The former was much the larger group in the general election of 1918 with 138 MPs returned and only 27 followers of Asquith, who was himself to lose his seat. This split was a major diversion for the Liberal Party at a critical and difficult time. The introduction of full universal suffrage for men and for women over thirty in 1918 would in any case have threatened the old Liberal/Conservative duopoly by greatly expanding the electorate at a time when the Labour Party was increasing in confidence and grassroots organisation. Significantly, in the 1918 election Labour returned 63 MPs on the basis of a new constitution and a clearly distinctive socialist programme.

In spite of not unsuccessful attempts to mend the split between the followers of Lloyd George and Asquith, the Liberal Party continued to suffer erosion of its electoral base. As a result the electoral history of the Liberal Party between the wars makes dismal reading. Its best performance was in the 1923 general election when Asquith and Lloyd George patched up their differences –

though Lloyd George maintained his own headquarters and control of funds – when the party gained 159 seats. But even this moderately respectable performance was overshadowed by the formation of a minority Labour government on the basis of 191 MPs: not only had the Labour Party overtaken the Liberals in parliamentary seats, but the Labour Party received its first taste of government with all the enhanced status and credibility that this brought with it. The last realistic chance that the Liberals had to bid for government came in 1929 when the party campaigned on a radical manifesto, Lloyd George's Yellow Book *We Can Conquer Unemployment*, containing ambitious proposals to conquer mass unemployment. The result, however, was profoundly discouraging with only 59 Liberals returned and, again, the formation of a Labour government.

The thirties saw continued decline for the Liberals at both parliamentary and local level. There were renewed splits, with some Liberals joining the National Government of 1931 and disagreement over whether Liberals could accept the policies of protection pursued by the National Government which to many seemed to be a flagrant breach with traditional Liberal policies of free trade. Lloyd George who, although old and ailing, was still in command of a sizeable political fund – in fact almost the only funds Liberals possessed – continued to play a maverick role with his own group of independent MPs and a still sizeable reputation as the most charismatic figure in the party. In the last general election before the Second World War, in 1935, the party which had governed Britain either alone or in coalition continuously between 1906 and 1922 was reduced to a mere 21 seats and less than 7 per cent of the total vote.

By the Second World War, the writing seemed on the wall for the Liberal Party. Beneath the sorry tale of splits and decline at parliamentary level lay the decay of grassroots organisation. While the Conservative Party under Baldwin and Chamberlain consolidated its position as the party of the shires and the urban middle class and Labour reinforced its hold on the industrial heartlands, the Liberals were quite literally being squeezed out and their support increasingly reduced to the Celtic fringe and a few independent bastions in rural and urban England. The Second World War did little to interrupt that decline. Although the Liberals took their place in the wartime coalition, there was little hiding the fact that any future electoral contest would be one in which they would have only a walk-on part. The powerful mood of social optimism and reconstruction which swept the country in the war years was one which favoured the Labour Party, not the Liberals. In the leftward shift amongst young intellectuals and writers of the late thirties, it was the Labour Party or even the Communist Party which was the principal beneficiary. Compared with the galaxy of talent which clustered around groups such as the Fabian Research Bureau and the Left Book Club, the Liberal Party seemed increasingly out-of-date and redundant. It did have one or two stars. Sir William Beveridge, the author of the famous report on Social Insurance in 1942 which set out the basis of the Welfare State, was a Liberal whose credentials went back to the Liberal heyday of the years before the Great War. So too, it is often forgotten, was John Maynard Keynes, whose economic ideas were to do so much to influence postwar economic policy. But these were chiefs without indians: the thousands of young men and women who voted for the first time in 1945, the children of the Slump, looked to the Labour Party, not the Liberals, to build the 'New Jerusalem'. In spite of some optimism on the part of the Liberals, the 1945 election result was a disaster. Only 12 Liberal MPs were returned and of the 475 Liberal candidates 319 – two-thirds – lost their deposits. The total Liberal share of the votes was just 9 per cent.

During the late forties and early fifties the leader of the Liberals, Clement Davies, was presiding over what was little more than the empty husk of a party, reduced to nine seats in 1950 and to six in 1951. In a sense Churchill, as the new Prime Minister in 1951, seemed only to be helping to put the party out of its misery when he offered its leader Clement Davies a place in government and *de facto* extinction as an independent political force. The offer was refused but to many observers it looked like a brave gesture from a dying man. In the 1955 election the party remained at six MPs; had less than three-quarters of a million votes; and accounted for less than 3 per cent of all votes cast. The party had only fielded 110 candidates of whom 60 lost their deposits. Put another way, Labour and the Conservatives between them now accounted for over 96 per cent of all votes cast. In the era of two-party dominance the Liberals were reduced to an irrelevant fringe. Nor was it only at Westminster that the Liberals were reduced. As a force in local government they were equally weak: only 2.2 per cent of councillors elected in 1950 were Liberal; by 1955 the figure was 1.5 per cent. At the local level as well as in parliament, the Liberals seemed to face extinction.

As often happens in politics, however, this nadir in Liberal fortunes preceded the first chink of light in the encircling gloom. In 1956 Clement Davies stood down as leader. Though worthy and respected, he had no power to revitalise the party. Moreover, the party was adrift in policy terms. All the progressive clothes it might have had had been stolen by Labour in the postwar years, and to those who were worried about the threat of socialism, an attractive option lay in voting for a Tory party led by decent liberal Tories like Eden and Macmillan. The fatal haemorrhage of Liberal votes to the Conservatives going on since the 1920s seemed virtually unstoppable, leaving the party with a handful of seats in Wales, Scotland and the West Country.

Davies, however, was succeeded by Jo Grimond, who quickly proved himself an attractive and vigorous leader. Aged only 43 in 1956, his seat in Orkney and Shetland gave him at least a secure basis from which to revitalise the party. It was Grimond who was gradually to fashion the idea of the Liberal Party as a party of the radical non-socialist left of centre, the position it has persistently claimed for itself ever since. Grimond was fortunate too in coming to the leadership just at a time when some disenchantment with the Conservative government was beginning to offer opportunities for the Liberals. Even before Grimond came to the leadership the Liberals had begun to score some impressive votes in parliamentary by-elections. Then, early in 1958, Ludovic Kennedy achieved a creditable second place at Rochdale with 35 per cent of the poll. Two weeks later at Torrington the Liberals obtained the by-election breakthrough that had eluded them for a generation when Mark Bonham-Carter won the seat from the Tories.

Liberal revival

The Torrington by-election marks the beginning of the second phase of Liberal politics since the Second World War. Where the years between 1945 and 1958 seemed only to continue the process of decline evident between the wars, after 1958 the party began a revival marked by a series of spectacular by-election results and a gradual increase in its share of the vote. Between 1929 and 1958 the party did not win a single by-election. After 1958 the party was to receive much needed publicity and welcome boosts to its confidence through its ability to overturn large majorities at by-elections. The party was entering the period when it could act as a vehicle for anti-government protest. But there was a more substantial basis to the Liberal revival shown in an increased share of the vote in the 1959 general election to 6 per cent and a doubling of its voting strength. In 1962 the party achieved another spectacular by-election success when Eric Lubbock won Orpington – the first Liberal breakthrough in the Conservative suburbs and a source of considerable optimism.

The history of the party in the sixties was a mixture of continued by-election successes, as in 1965 when David Steel won Roxburgh, Selkirk and Peebles, and a slow, painful increase in its share of the vote at general elections and the number of MPs elected: nine MPs in 1964, rising to 12 in 1966. However, the decade ended with a setback when in 1970 the party was reduced to only six seats and its vote fell, demonstrating the fragility of the Liberals as a parliamentary force. None the less, with over two million votes, the party was clearly reviving from its near-extinction in the fifties. One problem for the Liberals at a Parliamentary level was that by the late sixties they were being challenged in their heartland, the Celtic fringe, by the rise of the Welsh and Scottish Nationalist Parties who threatened to steal from the Liberals the only areas where they had been able to maintain some kind of electoral base. Moreover, the party still lacked a clear identity for many voters. Its capacity to act as a vehicle for protest was not yet matched by its ability to project a distinctive positive image at a general election in competition with the other main parties. Almost in recognition of this, Jo Grimond resigned as leader in 1967 with many commentators arguing that his dream of a radical alternative to Labour had, in fact, failed to materialise. The paradox was that where the Liberals seemed best able to capture new votes was as an alternative middle-class vote in suburban, Tory-held seats – it remained an almost total failure in its assault on Labour-controlled areas.

The new leader in 1967 was Jeremy Thorpe. Once again the party had chosen a young leader, aged only 38. Educated, like

Grimond, at Oxford, he was a trained lawyer and a presentable television and media performer. But the late sixties brought an even younger generation of Liberals to the fore. One by-product of the student activism of the decade was an infusion of radical young people into the party. The Young Liberals began a pronounced leftward trend which caused considerable discomfort for the staid, older generation. As an example, in 1966 the Young Liberals were demanding the withdrawal of all American troops from Vietnam; workers' control of nationalised industries; non-alignment in the cold war, British withdrawal from NATO; opposition to the wage freeze; support for majority rule in Rhodesia; and active support for the anti-apartheid movement. But besides causing a certain amount of internal party strife, there were some lasting results. The Young Liberals placed increasing emphasis on what was known as 'community politics'; direct action campaigns and support for local issues of the most banal kind, sometimes dubbed 'pothole and pavement' politics, provided an outlet for activists. It brought the Liberals into the forefront of one of the most potent sociopolitical movements of the late sixties and early seventies, the development of grassroots organisations such as tenants' groups, community associations, and conservation lobbies. The growth of these forces was part of a growing disillusionment with the excesses of bureaucracy and the crassness of planning, increasingly highlighted by the housing and redevelopment boom of the sixties and early seventies. At the local level Liberals were also able to take advantage of the decay and complacency of the major parties, particularly in urban areas. The 'Focus' leaflet and community newsletter became the hallmark of much local campaigning. An important result of this was that the Liberals began to build up a strong base of local councillors in places like Liverpool, Leeds and Birmingham. Decayed and moribund local Labour parties, as in Liverpool, soon found themselves facing powerful groupings of Liberal councillors.

For a moment in 1974 it appeared that the Liberals might even be on the verge of a breakthrough into parliamentary power. A series of dramatic by-election victories in 1972–3 were followed by the Liberals winning fourteen seats in the 1974 election, obtaining over six million votes, a fifth of all votes cast. More importantly, the defeated Prime Minister Edward Heath opened talks about a coalition with the Liberals in order to preserve his government in power, but these broke down with Heath's refusal to promise electoral reform. The chance of a place in government was gone almost as soon as it had appeared. The Liberals remained out of power. Then, in 1976, they were rocked by a highly damaging scandal surrounding their leader Jeremy Thorpe, forcing his resignation and casting the party once again into the doldrums.

Following an interregnum leadership by Jo Grimond and David Steel, Steel was elected leader through the operation of a newly devised Electoral College – the first leader of a British political party in the twentieth century to be elected by democratic means. Steel's election as a fresh, young leader with impeccable credentials as a 'son of the manse' finally buried the Thorpe affair. Less obvious than Steel's clean-cut image, however, was the skilled politician who was determined to take the opportunity of the weakness of the ruling Labour government to give the Liberal Party some share of power and the discipline of responsibility. In 1977 he was given a chance when the ailing administration of James Callaghan sought a pact with the Liberals. The so-called Lib-Lab pact gave the Liberals a consultative role in government, but no seats in Cabinet nor any firm promise of proportional representation. Many Liberals believed a better deal could have been struck and there was much criticism of the pact at grassroots level. By 1978 the pact was over, the Liberals having failed to secure proportional representation even in the first direct European elections which some had hoped was a minimum that could have been demanded.

When the Labour government fell in 1979 following the Winter of Discontent the Liberals found themselves smeared by their association with the Labour Party. The party only returned eleven MPs and its vote fell by two million to 14 per cent of votes cast. The revival seemed stalled.

The age of alliance

Margaret Thatcher's victory in 1979, however, brought about a new and promising development for the Liberals. Labour's defeat brought to a head the strains in the party and the bitter conflicts between left and right. The defection of the 'Gang of Four' and the formation of the Social Democratic Party in March 1981 marked the beginning of the third phase of postwar Liberal politics. When in September 1981 an Alliance between the Liberals and the SDP was formed, for the first time it appeared that a credible third force in British politics was established. The SDP brought experienced ex-cabinet ministers, 21 MPs, new members – 66,000 by the end of 1981 – and new enthusiasm. By early 1982, with Labour in disarray and the Thatcher government deeply unpopular because of its economic policy, some opinion polls were predicting an Alliance victory at the polls. The Alliance was assisted by the old Liberal standby, some spectacular and headline-grabbing by-election victories, notably Shirley Williams at Crosby in November 1981 and Roy Jenkins at Glasgow Hillhead in March 1982. For a moment it seemed the Alliance could sweep all before it, but the Falklands War in spring 1982 put the Conservatives back into a commanding lead in the opinion polls. When the 1983 election was held the results were a bitter disappointment – only 23 Alliance MPs were returned even though the vote at almost eight million – almost a quarter of votes cast – was the highest recorded since 1923.

The Alliance remained in a frustrating position between 1983 and 1987. While it consolidated its position in local government and was frequently able to score spectacular successes in parliamentary by-elections, its credibility as an alternative governing party remained in doubt. David Owen's assumption of the leadership of the SDP in place of Roy Jenkins created difficulties. A dominant personality both in the media and in Parliament, it was clear that Owen, as well as having his own strong views on issues such as defence and economic policy, took seriously the idea of the SDP as an independent and distinct entity and was opposed to a merger with the Liberals. During the summer and autumn of 1986 disagreements over defence policy threatened a major rift in the Alliance. The strong unilateralist and pacifist elements in the Liberal Party, only just held at bay by the leadership in previous years, were increasingly annoyed by what they saw as the pre-emption of nuclear policy by David Owen and apparent compliance by David Steel in discussion of a new generation of nuclear deterrent based on a 'Euro-bomb'. The resulting revolt of the Liberal Assembly at Eastbourne in September 1986, passing a non-nuclear amendment on defence policy in defiance of the party leadership, brought this rift into the open. Its effects on the standing of the Alliance in the opinion polls were disastrous, demonstrating again the fragility of Alliance support. Although a compromise defence policy was patched up by the New Year in time for a relaunch of the Alliance, the underlying tensions over defence and the dual leadership of the Alliance proved fatal handicaps to the Alliance in the 1987 election campaign. The failure of the Alliance bandwagon ever to gather momentum and the modest turn-out for the party in terms of share of the vote, slightly less than in 1983, with only twenty-two MPs returned, pointed to the need to reappraise the whole future of the Alliance. Reappraisal, however, was precipitated more swiftly than almost anyone expected by David Steel's call for a merger immediately following the declaration of the election result. David Owen's no less swift declaration against merger and a call for a ballot of the SDP membership on the issue brought matters to a bitter and painful climax. Following a vote by the SDP in favour of merger talks, David Owen's resignation of the leadership of the SDP in favour of Robert MacLennan left the way clear for a protracted and far from smooth process of negotiating the merger of the two parties. After high drama and a hastily redrafted statement of policies, votes at special conferences of the Liberals and SDP in January left the way open for the launch of the new Social and Liberal Democrats in March 1988.

The new party immediately faced two tests. The first was the local elections of May 1988, with the successor party to the Alliance slumping in the polls and barely ahead of David Owen's reconstituted 'continuing' SDP. As anticipated, the new SLD lost ground, with a net loss of over sixty council seats; but taken over the broad spectrum of seats being defended, the losses were fairly marginal and the party had secured a vote considerably better than its current opinion poll ratings. More encouragingly, the weakness of the 'continuing' SDP was ruthlessly exposed, defending only a fraction of the seats of the SLD and losing heavily. The second was the question of leadership, held in abeyance until after the local elections had been fought. Following the local elections, as widely anticipated, David Steel declared that he would not be a candidate for the leadership. By the opening of the eight-week election campaign in June 1988, the two candidates were Paddy Ashdown and Alan Beith. In a series of 'hustings meetings' up and down the country, it soon became apparent that there were few differences of principle between the candidates: more ones of personality and strategy. Ashdown's insistence that the SLD must replace the Labour Party was met by Beith's argument that such a strategy was unrealistic. The outcome, however, was a decisive victory for Ashdown by six votes to one.

Meanwhile the opinion polls were registering a major loss of public support for both the old Alliance partners, putting them at less than half of their rating in the general election 12 months earlier. While the leadership contest was underway the SLD and continuing SDP faced their first Parliamentary by-election at Kensington. Neither emerged very creditably: the SLD was unable to repeat anything like the spectacular bandwagon effect of earlier by-elections, its only crumb of comfort being that the SDP candidate obtained fewer votes and almost lost his deposit.

The first conferences since the breakup of the Alliance were eagerly awaited to see how the ex-partners would fare. The SDP's conference at Torquay (September 1988) was notable for David Owen's clear declaration that his party would continue and his espousal of the issue of electoral reform as a main plank in SDP's programme. The SLD conference at Blackpool (September 1988) was immediately pitched into a passionate debate about the short name by which the party would be known. To the evident dismay of some ex-Liberals, a clear majority accepted the title of Democrats. With by- and Euro-elections pending, however, the future of the old Alliance partners still appeared to hang in the balance and ultimately to be decided by the electorate. The Epping Forest and Richmond by-elections confirmed that the SDP could frustrate the mobilisation of third-party support by the Democrats, but it was a fresh force, the Greens, which proved the greatest threat in 1989. While the SDP withdrew as a national force after the local elections in May, the Greens swept to a stunning success in the Euro-elections in June, pushing the Democrats into a humiliating fourth place in the total vote and ensuring numerous lost deposits. By autumn, with opinion polls showing the lowest level of support since the 1950s, and overtaken by the Greens, fresh dissent about the Party name, and a financial crisis, the Democrats faced an uphill struggle to re-establish themselves as a credible force.

Retrospect

In over two years of considerable turmoil since the 1987 election, the prospect for a 'third force' in British politics has been dramatically reshaped. The old Liberal Party has, in fact, ceased to exist, ending its long independent history and has merged its identity along with the majority of the activists, councillors and MPs of the seven-year-old SDP in the Social and Liberal Democrats. What the future holds is difficult to predict, but a review of the strengths and weaknesses of the Liberal Party revealed by its history since 1945 might suggest some clues. First, the survival of the Liberal Party to become a major component of a new political party was not a foregone conclusion. Its revival from near-extinction in the immediate postwar years represents one of the most remarkable political about-turns of the century. In a reversal of the process of apparently ineluctable decline witnessed for much of the first half of the century, the record since 1955 has been of revival, even if not to its pre-1914 strength, then well beyond that prior to 1945. Second, the history of the Liberal Party and then the Alliance demonstrates the disadvantage of any third party in Britain under the present electoral system. Although the Alliance obtained approximately a quarter of all votes cast in 1983 and 1987, it obtained only a score or more members of Parliament. The problem of a first-past-the-post system for any minority party was compounded by the even spread and volatility of Alliance support, so that it was unable to count upon a bloc of 'safe' seats in the way Labour did in its industrial heartlands or the Conservatives did in the southeast of England. It has been calculated that even if Labour's support fell to 20 per cent at some future general election it would still have about 150 MPs because of the concentration of its vote; with a larger percentage share of the vote in both 1983 and 1987 the Liberals and their Alliance partners could muster a bare two dozen. In so far as the Liberal Party has had its bastions, these have remained in the Celtic fringe, the Southwest, Wales and Scotland from which it still draws a disproportionate number of its MPs. Even so, if for example, one asks which seat has been held permanently by the Liberals this century, the answer is none. Third, any minority party working within the adversarial tradition of British politics, where the place of government and opposition is enshrined in the procedures of Parliament and reinforced in the attitudes of the media, operates at a disadvantage. The Liberal Party has therefore been heavily dependent upon by-election successes to raise its public visibility and earn it the media attention it otherwise lacks. As a third party operating in a two-party situation, the Liberals have frequently found themselves denied the 'oxygen of publicity' which any modern party requires, and gasping for air in the lulls between by-elections. This has led many to the conclusion that it is only by replacing one of the other major parties that any 'third force' can achieve a breakthrough.

Certainly at parliamentary level, the fortunes of the Liberal Party can be shown to have been dependent in large part upon the state of the other parties. The Liberal revival took off in the late fifties amidst the disillusion with the Conservative government of Macmillan; its point of greatest, if illusory, success came when both major parties were in the doldrums in the early eighties. At parliamentary level, the Liberal and now the SLD nightmare is of a strong Conservative Party faced by a revived Labour Party, maintaining a fatal 'squeeze' upon its electoral prospects. Fourth, however, and more encouraging, is the way the Liberals, the Alliance and then the SLD have established a major foothold in local government. With over three thousand local councillors, they have been much more successful in establishing an apparently permanent power base in local government in both rural and urban areas. SLD councillors control areas as diverse as Tower Hamlets in London, Stockport, Hereford, Plymouth, and Blythe Valley in the Northeast. In an even larger number of counties they hold the balance of power. Moreover, there is a clear discrepancy between local election results and national opinion polls. It seems that whenever people actually vote, they tend to be more favourably disposed to a third force than their answers to pollsters would indicate. Fifth, what of policy? Since 1945 the Liberal Party has always found it difficult to establish an identity sufficiently distinctive from that of the two major parties. Even when its revival began in the late fifties it was easy to argue that it was no more than a 'protest' party and as recently as the 1987 election one of the commonest complaints of electors was that they did not know what the Alliance 'stood for'. In many ways, however, the Liberal Party has been more important as a source of ideas which have entered the mainstream of political debate than as a vehicle for carrying them out. It is worth remembering that it was a young

David Steel who sponsored the introduction of the Abortion Act in 1967. Liberals have also championed devolution and regionalism; they have campaigned for proportional representation and for industrial democracy, as well as for a Bill of Rights and a Freedom of Information Act. Internal party structures both in the Alliance partners and the new SLD have set new standards for participatory democracy in British political parties with direct election of the leader on the basis of 'one member one vote' and a democratic system of policy creation. As a means of putting new ideas on the political agenda, the Liberal Party and its successors have had more influence than their number of MPs would suggest. It would, however, be appropriate to end on a question mark about what identity the new party will seek for itself. Will it be a centre party, drawing its votes from disgruntled Conservatives as well as defectors from Labour or, as Grimond's vision had it, an alternative radical party of the left, ultimately supplanting Labour as the progressive anti-Conservative party in British politics? What is clear is that with an SLD under new leadership, the rise of the Greens, and a Labour Party seeking to modernise itself, a major realignment is taking place in the centre and centre-left of British politics. Whatever the outcome might be, it seems likely that the beneficiaries of the Liberal Party's long march from near-extinction might still have a part to play – but how great remains to be seen.

Key dates, 1945–89

1945	July	Liberals win twelve seats in general election. Clement Davies elected chairman of parliamentary party.
1950	Feb.	Nine Liberal MPs returned in general election; 319 of 475 Liberal candidates lose their deposits.
1951	May	Six Liberals returned at general election. Churchill offers Clement Davies the Ministry of Education. He declines the offer.
1956		Davies resigns leadership. Jo Grimond elected chairman of the Liberal MPs.
1958	Mar.	Mark Bonham-Carter wins Torrington by-election, first Liberal by-election victory since 1929.
1959	Oct.	Liberals win six seats at general election.
1962	Mar.	Eric Lubbock wins Orpington by-election.
1964	Oct.	Liberals win nine seats in general election.
1965	Mar.	David Steel wins Roxburgh, Selkirk and Peebles by-election.

1966	Mar.	Liberals win twelve seats in general election.
1967		Grimond resigns. Jeremy Thorpe elected chairman of Liberal MPs.
1970	June	Liberals win six seats in general election.
1972–3		Dramatic series of Liberal by-election victories in Rochdale, Sutton, Ely, Ripon and Berwick.
1974	Feb.	Liberals win fourteen seats in general election; Heath approaches Thorpe with offer of a coalition but talks break down when Heath refuses to promise electoral reform.
	Oct.	Liberals win thirteen seats in general election.
1976		Thorpe resigns after party pressure following the Norman Scott scandal. 'Interregnum' leadership by Grimond and Steel until Steel elected leader of the party.
1977		Liberals enter Lib-Lab pact to sustain minority Callaghan government.
1978		Liberals withdraw from Lib-Lab pact.
1979	May	Liberals win eleven seats in general election.
1981	Mar.	Formation of the Social Democratic Party.
	Sept.	Liberals and SDP form Alliance.
1983	June	Alliance win 26 per cent of the vote in the general election but only 23 seats.
1986	Sept.	Eastbourne Conference passes non-nuclear amendment in opposition to leadership; Alliance slumps in polls.
1987	June	Alliance wins 22 seats in the general election with 23 per cent of the vote. David Steel immediately calls for a merger of the two parties; David Owen opposes merger and resigns as leader of the SDP.
1988	Jan.	Liberal and SDP special conferences vote for merger of the two parties and formation of the Social and Liberal Democrats.
	Mar.	Launch of the new Social and Liberal Democrats. David Owen forms 'continuing SDP'.
	June	David Steel announces he will not stand in forthcoming leadership contest.
	July	Ashdown elected leader of Social and Liberal Democrats.
	Sept.	Social and Liberal Democrats and 'continuing SDP' have separate conferences.
1989	Feb.	SDP take second place over SLD at Richmond by-election.
	June	Greens push SLD into fourth place in Euro-elections and overtake them in the opinion polls.
	Aug.	Major financial crisis in SLD; regional staff disbanded, HQ staff halved.

4

The Social Democratic Party, 1981–88

GERARD DALY

> Every Centre is divided against itself and remains separated into
> two halves, Left-Centre and Right-Centre. For the Centre is
> nothing more than the artificial grouping of the right wing of the
> Left and the left wing of the Right. The fate of the Centre is to be
> torn asunder, buffeted and annihilated: torn asunder when one of
> its halves votes Right and the other Left, buffeted when it votes as
> a group first Right then Left, annihilated when it abstains from
> voting. The dream of the Centre is to achieve a synthesis of
> contradictory aspirations; but synthesis is a power only of the mind.
>
> (M. Duverger, *Political Parties,* p. 215, 3rd edn, 1964)

The Social Democratic Party was launched in the Connaught
Rooms, London, on 26 March 1981. It had a short life, but an
eventful one, and its ending was as acrimonious as its beginning.
The events of 1981 were the most damaging for the Labour Party
since the split in 1931 and the secession of National Labour
supporters led by Ramsay Macdonald. But unlike National Labour
in the thirties, the SDP aimed at a sustained electoral challenge to
the Labour Party with a sophisticated party machinery and large
membership in the country. The electoral consequence of a rival
contender for anti-Conservative votes was manifested in major
defeats for Labour in the 1983 and 1987 general elections. The
events of 1981 had effects from which the Labour Party has not
yet recovered.

Origins

But what was the SDP all about? Was it just a splinter or did it represent something more? Two factors lay behind its foundation. The first was that of a reaction against increased left-wing power inside the Labour Party. This resulted in a sizeable group, but not all, of Labour's social democrats led by three ex-cabinet ministers, Dr David Owen, Shirley Williams, and William Rodgers (described as the Gang of Three) leaving the party. Their dismay with the leftward drift of Labour policy in the aftermath of the 1979 election defeat made them want to form a party which would be a more acceptable alternative to Mrs Thatcher. They believed that a left-wing Labour Party would be unelectable. In this sense, the Labour breakaways were united by being against the rise of the Labour left. Having seemingly lost the intra-party struggle against the left, that struggle was now to be engaged in electoral rivalry. The second factor was a more positive one: that of a realignment of British politics. Roy Jenkins, a former deputy leader of the Labour Party, in his Dimbleby Lecture of 22 November 1979, argued for the need for a new centre party. Such a party would have a programme of radical social and constitutional reform and would marginalise Labour without becoming its Mark II variant in order to achieve this. The new party would aim to attract support from left and right as well as from those who previously were not involved in politics.

Supporters of the idea of a new party pointed to electoral evidence, with a number of studies suggesting a constituency of support for a party of the centre which went beyond existing confines of Liberal Party support. Crewe and Sarlvik's *Decade of Dealignment* (1983) identified a decline in electoral support for the Labour Party, with voters disliking the link with the trade unions and nationalisation. On its own, the Liberal Party achieved nearly one-fifth of the vote in the February and October 1974 general elections. After the election defeat of 1979 discontent among Labour moderates found expression in the centre-right pressure group founded by Ian Wrigglesworth, John Cartwright, William Rodgers and Alec McGivan in 1977, called the Campaign for Labour Victory. Initially concerned with organisational reform and modernisation, CLV increasingly became the forum for discussion about a breakaway from the Labour Party, and contained within its ranks individuals who were subsequently to play a leading role in the SDP. As the Labour left won important constitutional and policy changes at the 1979 and 1980 conferences, so the idea of a new party gained appeal. The Gang of Three published an appeal to Labour Party members in *The Guardian* on 1 August 1980 which hinted at the possibility of a breakaway: 'if the Labour Party abandons its democratic and internationalist principles, the argument may grow for a new democratic socialist party to establish itself as a party of conscience and reform committed to those principles.'

The election of Michael Foot, a long-standing supporter of unilateral nuclear disarmament and member of the left-wing Tribune Group, as Labour leader on 10 November 1980 was one of the decisive factors leading to the split. Foot failed to reassure the Labour moderates and lacked the leadership skill required for preventing a split. In addition to this, a split opened up on the Labour right itself between those who wanted to leave the party and those who decided to stay. Before the Wembley Special Conference on 24 January 1981 to decide the method of electing the Labour leader, the Manifesto Group of moderate Labour MPs met on 15 January. At this meeting Dr Owen and his supporters, who wanted a split, clashed with Roy Hattersley and his larger group of followers who wanted to stay. Dr Owen insisted that one member one vote was the only acceptable alternative method of electing the leader. Roy Hattersley, meanwhile, had accepted the principle of an electoral college and wanted Labour MPs to have the largest share of votes in this. The meeting polarised on this issue. Roy Hattersley withdrew his support from CLV after this meeting. The meeting was also significant because it prevented a larger body of discontented MPs from joining Dr Owen in his prospective split.

Having lost the one member one vote option, and with conference voting to give trade unions the largest share in the new electoral college, the Gang of Three and their supporters put into action plans they had been developing in detail since Christmas. On 25 January 1981 they issued the Limehouse Declaration and set up an interim body called the Council for Social Democracy. Nine Labour MPs immediately declared their support for the Council, and the support of one hundred distinguished individuals was published in *The Guardian* on 5 February. The pressure to launch the new party as early as possible led to it being launched on 26 March.

There are three themes running through the subsequent short history of the SDP. The first is a struggle for electoral credibility, and this involves looking at the organisation and strategy of the party. The second theme is a search for identity as either a left of centre party to replace Labour, or something different, new. If so, what? The third theme is that of the increasingly serious internal struggle between Owenites and the rest over merger with the Liberal Party. From the beginning there was a difference in attitude to the Liberal partners in the Alliance, and this was not to be resolved and was to be the cause of many set-backs in the party's fortunes as well as leading to its demise in the way and at the time it did.

Organisation, strategy, and intra-party democracy

The SDP worked quickly to establish its credibility with the electorate as a viable political party by launching a massive membership recruitment drive. Advertisements appeared in newspapers and people interested in joining could pay by credit card. Apart from the financial backing of a small group of wealthy businessmen such as David Sainsbury, the SDP relied on income from membership fees to support itself. Membership reached a level of around 70,000 and remained around this figure until after the 1987 general election. The SDP boasted that it had the most democratic constitution of all political parties. The reality is more complicated. The Gang of Four and the steering committee was self-appointed until the leadership election in July 1982, and the election of the National Committee at the autumn 1982 conference, itself the first conference with elected representatives (the 1981 assembly was 'consultative' and consisted of activists willing to attend). Moreover, the principle of one member one vote was hotly contested at the Kensington Convention on the Party Constitution held on 13 February 1982. Two members of the Gang of Four, Roy Jenkins and William Rodgers, were in favour of the leader being elected by MPs only. David Owen spoke in favour of one member one vote, and the decision in favour of this option was won by 166 votes but with a substantial minority of 73 votes against. The SDP constitution was highly centralised with a London-based National Committee of thirty-nine members and three co-options, twelve members of which were elected by the Council for Social Democracy and eight elected by the national membership. Candidates for election to the National Committee were not allowed to make policy statements and instead were limited to biographical details only. This tended to have the effect that candidates were elected on the basis of how well-known they were rather than of their policy stance. Thus, journalists such as Polly Toynbee and Anthony Sampson were elected.

The Council for Social Democracy was the policy-making assembly of the SDP. Area parties elected representatives to serve for a period of two years, when there would be new elections. The Policy Subcommittee, elected by the National Committee, had the real power. It established policy working groups which would publish consultative Green Papers and then submit a White Paper for approval by the Council. The Council could vote on resolutions and amendments submitted by Area Parties in response to the Policy White Papers. Unlike the Labour Party Conference where delegations could be mandated to vote a particular way, the members of the Council were constitutionally precluded from any mandate as to how they would vote. In theory, the degree of Council power seems impressive. In practice, the Council was a rather tame body, invariably following the recommendations of the platform. Exceptions do exist. At the first CSD in Great Yarmouth in September 1982, the Council voted against a statutory incomes policy (backed by Jenkins) and opted instead for a voluntary one, as proposed in a motion put forward by Ruth Levitt, a former research assistant to David Owen. At the Buxton Council in September 1984, the floor voted against the platform in favour of an emergency motion against the use of plastic bullets in Northern Ireland. In this case the platform decided to ignore this policy and had the decision subsequently reversed.

The parliamentary party and the leadership enjoyed considerable autonomy from activist control. Cohesion in the remainder of the 1979–83 Parliament was difficult to maintain. The parliamentary SDP was split over its attitude to the Employment Bill, some MPs supporting legislation to curb trade union power, others thought that Conservative proposals went too far. In May 1982 the Group decided to abstain on the Third Reading of Norman Tebbit's Employment Bill. This was different from the Liberal position, which was to support the Bill. The handful of SDP MPs elected in the 1983 (six) and 1987 (five) general elections saw a truncated Parliamentary wing, and this made necessary the need for strong leadership if the SDP were not to disappear from public view completely.

This was the source of the trend towards leader dominance inside the SDP. Roy Jenkins, having won the Glasgow Hillhead by-election on 25 March 1982, was able to stand against Dr Owen in the leadership election of that year. Jenkins had a chairman-like style and preferred to strengthen the Alliance with the Liberal Party rather than asserting a personal mark on SDP affairs. He was given the hapless title of 'prime minister designate' in the 1983 Alliance campaign in the general election. His image and perform-ance in that election led to criticism by campaign strategists and a lower profile for the second half of the campaign. The June 1983 election saw a depleted parliamentary party, and Jenkins, returned as MP for Hillhead, resigned. As there was no other candidate for the leadership, Dr Owen succeeded Jenkins as leader automatically.

Owen displayed a skill at grabbing media attention beyond proportion to the SDP's size in parliament. However, this began to raise the problem of the leader taking on too much power as more and more policy seemed to be made by pronouncements from Dr Owen pre-empting decisions of his party conference. As a firm opponent of merger, he succeeded in preventing a merger after the 1983 election, with a motion in favour of merger rejected at the Salford conference in September 1983. At the 1984 and 1985 autumn Councils, Dr Owen outlined in his speeches his 'tough but tender' approach to Britain's problems, and advocated a 'social market economy' of a mix between minimal welfare standards and minimal state interventionism in the economy. Dr Owen's power base grew as leader, having a majority on the National Committee and a key ally in Mike Thomas as Chairman of the Organisation Committee. However, defeat in the ballot on whether to hold merger talks after the 1987 general election caused Dr Owen to resign as leader, and the SDP spent some weeks without a leader until a caretaker leader in Robert MacLennan was found to see the party through the merger negotiations.

Electoral strategy

The SDP throughout remained undecided as to whether it should displace the Labour Party as the main opposition to the Conservatives – and so target only Labour votes – or aim at winning through the middle by taking Conservative and Labour votes. Each strategy had different requirements. The former required policies to attract Labour voters and the targeting of Labour seats. The problem with this was that the SDP was not organisationally or electorally strong enough to mount a challenge in Labour's strongholds in the North and in Scotland and Wales. On the contrary, the SDP was strong in those seats held by Conservatives and to win required gaining Conservative, and not Labour, votes, Labour having been squeezed to its bedrock. The victory of the SDP candidate, Rosie Barnes, in the Greenwich by-election in February 1987 was the only occasion when the SDP succeeded in winning a by-election from a Labour-held seat, and this was largely due to Conservative votes swinging behind the SDP as the party best able to defeat Labour. The latter strategy of attracting Conservative votes became necessary; but this entailed the watering down of more radical commitments (such as its tax and benefits proposals which the party moderated before the 1987 election) so as to be palatable to Conservative voters.

The SDP did not fare as well in parliamentary by-elections as did the Liberals. In the period before the 1983 general election, the SDP did well in the Warrington by-election in July 1981, coming a close second in a former safe Labour seat, but lost the Mitcham and Morden by-election, held on 3 June 1982, and did badly in Darlington in March 1983, with Tony Cook, a weak candidate, coming a poor third despite initial predictions of an SDP landslide. After Darlington the SDP amended its constitution to allow the reselection of a more able candidate to cope with extensive media attention. In the 1983–7 parliament the SDP made little progress, winning Portsmouth South in June 1984 (and losing it in the 1987 general election), and coming a poor third in the Fulham by-election in March 1986. In local government the SDP fared better, with Anne Sofer holding on to her seat on the GLC in a by-election in October 1981, and SDP gains in the 1982 local elections and 1985 Shire County elections. However, the first ever SDP controlled council, formed in December 1981 by defecting Labour councillors, in Islington, London, had a short period in office when it was removed in the May 1982 London Borough elections.

Ideology and policy

If the SDP failed to establish a solid electoral base of its own at the expense of Labour, it also had an inconclusive search for an identity. The search went in phases: first neo-Croslandism, then radical-centrism, then a brief flirtation in 1984 and 1985 with the philosophy of John Rawls, and concurrent with this, Dr Owen's 'social market economy'. The SDP policy machine was active very early with the appointment of Christopher Smallwood as Policy Co-ordinator in August 1981 (succeeded after the 1983 general election by Wendy Buckley) and numerous policy documents were prepared for each of the Council meetings. The policy documents are notable for their managerialist approach and wealth of detail, but no clear message. Attention was also focused on ideology. The Tawney Society was launched by Michael Young on 25 January 1982 as the party's think tank. Its first conference was held in Croydon, south London, on 13 March 1982. The Limehouse Group was established in July 1984 by Richard Gravil, Mike Slavin and Will Fitzgerald in response to the perceived rightward drift of SDP policy and a desire to return to the radical principles of the Limehouse Declaration of January 1981. At the 1985 autumn Council in Torquay the relationship of the SDP with socialism and Labour values was discussed. The Council asserted the distinctiveness of social democracy from socialism and dissociated itself from 'Labour values'. Torquay was widely regarded by Social Democrats as their most successful Council, and opinion polls witnessed a rise in support for a selfconfident SDP. However, the SDP was not to embrace the 'social market economy' philosophy of Dr Owen and his supporters, as a motion from its leading proponent, Anthony Goodman (Harrow Area Party) was rejected by the Council which met at Portsmouth in September 1987. Critics inside and outside the SDP have seen little difference between Dr Owen's ideas on the 'social market economy' and the neo-liberal economic policies of Ludwig Erhard of the German Christian Democratic Party in the 1950s.

To merge or not to merge?

The development of SDP ideology and policy took place within, and was constrained by, an alliance with the Liberal Party, approved in the autumn of 1981. From the beginning of the SDP's life the question of merger with the Liberal Party was not far away. Prior to forming the SDP, co-founder Roy Jenkins approached Liberal leader, David Steel, seeking to join the Liberals. David Steel believed that his aim of a realignment in British politics would best be served by the formation of a new party. The problems of two parties working together were enormous. In 1981 a crisis over the share-out of seats threatened to end the Alliance. Joint policy and joint strategy committees had to be formed. There was also the problem of two leaders, made worse after David Owen became leader of the SDP because of his desire for a distinct SDP identity. Thus in the 1987 general election, media attention focused on the divisions between the two leaders. However, the most serious problem for the SDP was the Liberal policy on defence, and the unilateralism often declared in votes at the Liberal Assemblies. An Alliance Defence Commission was set up after the 1983 election to formulate a joint defence policy for the next election. Before the Report of the Commission was published in the summer of 1986, Dr Owen made a speech in which he insisted that 'Britain must remain a nuclear weapons state'. He attacked the Commission's Report as a 'fudge' for postponing any decision about whether or not to replace Polaris when it came up for decommissioning in the mid-1990s. Dr Owen sparked a major row with the Party's President, Shirley Williams, who insisted that the leader did not necessarily speak for SDP policy (*The Times,* 7 July 1986). At the Liberal Assembly in Eastbourne in the autumn of 1986 the Commission's proposal on postponing a decision on Polaris was rejected in favour of a unilateralist position. The damage inflicted on the Alliance was not to heal, despite attempts to reconcile the two positions with the notion of a Euro-bomb. Unlike September 1983 when the SDP voted against merger with the Liberal Party, the SDP after the 1987 election voted 57.4 per cent in favour of merger talks in a ballot declared on 6 August. However, a sizeable body of SDP members refused to join in merger talks, and an embryonic new party was formed in December 1987 called the Campaign for Social Democracy. After the Council voted at Sheffield on 31 January by 273 in favour of merger and only 28 against with 49 abstentions, the merger was approved by the membership in the ballot declared on 2 March

1988. While 65.3 per cent were in favour of merger, a third of the membership, 34.7 per cent, was against. The Campaign for Social Democracy became the 'continuing SDP' with the same constitution as that of the original SDP when the SDP formally merged to form the Social and Liberal Democrats.

Conclusion

The SDP was weakened by the absence of a strategy and direction, failed to achieve an identity, and was internally divided over merger with the Liberals – the issue which paralysed the party in the last few months of its existence. The aim of a realignment was not realised, but its existence helped make a number of things happen. First, it acted as an electoral constraint on the Labour Party, providing it with every incentive to moderate itself or maybe lose support to the SDP. The split in 1981 had a sobering effect on the Labour Party, as was evidenced by the loss of the left-wing majority on the National Executive Committee at the 1981 Conference, and continuing modifications in policy under Neil Kinnock. Second, the SDP attracted a slice of Labour support and support from those with no previous party affiliation to add to the existing support for the Liberal Party, and which brought it within half a million votes of overtaking Labour in the 1983 election. Lastly, the SDP was an experimental ground for the modernisation of political parties with the introduction of credit card subscriptions, direct mailing to members, and the use of computer technology to target voters in by-elections.

Nevertheless, the Conservatives remained in power and the SDP did not displace the Labour Party. Now merged into the Social and Liberal Democrats, it makes another attempt at realignment. The experience of the SDP is of interest because it represented an attempt to bring together into one grouping in the political centre (with the Liberal Party), centrists from both the Labour and Conservative parties. It also shows the resilience of the Conservative and Labour parties in holding on to their centrists, thus maintaining the two-party system and the absence of an institutionalised centre party within reach of a majority in the House of Commons.

Bibliography

Bradley, I. (1981) *Breaking the Mould,* Martin Robertson.
Harris, K. (1987) *David Owen: Personally Speaking,* Weidenfeld & Nicolson.
Owen, D. (1981) *Face the Future,* Cape.
Owen, D. and Steel, D. (1987) *The Time Has Come,* Weidenfeld & Nicolson.
Rawls, John (1973) *A Theory of Justice,* Oxford University Press.
Rodgers, W. (1982) *The Politics of Change,* Secker & Warburg.
Stephenson, H. (1982) *Claret and Chips,* Michael Joseph.
Williams, S. (1981) *Politics is for People,* Penguin.
Wilson, D. (1987) *Battle for Power,* Sphere.

Key dates

1981	25 Jan.	Limehouse Declaration.
	26 Mar.	Launch of SDP.
	16 June	Joint policy declaration by SDP and Liberal Party, *A Fresh Start for Britain.*
	16 July	Warrington by-election.
	4–9 Oct.	SDP Conference Perth, Bradford and London.
	26 Nov.	Shirley Williams elected MP for Crosby.
1982	25 Jan.	Launch of Tawney Society.
	13 Feb.	Kensington Convention on the Constitution.
	25 Mar.	Glasgow Hillhead by-election elects Roy Jenkins MP.
	2 July	Jenkins defeats Owen in leadership contest.
	15–16 Oct.	First meeting of Council for Social Democracy, Great Yarmouth.
1983	24 Mar.	Darlington by-election, SDP a poor third.
	May	Alliance manifesto, *Working Together for Britain.*
	9 June	General election. SDP reduced to six MPs.
		Owen takes over as leader.
	11–14 Sept.	Salford Council rejects merger with Liberals.
1984	14 June	Michael Hancock wins Portsmouth South by-election for SDP.
	9–12 Sept.	Buxton Council defies platform by voting against use of plastic bullets in Northern Ireland.
		David Owen outlines 'social market' approach.
1985	2 May	Shire County elections – gains for SDP.
	7–11 Sept.	Torquay Council defeats motion on Labour values.
1986	Mar.	Fulham by-election – SDP a poor third.
	Aug.	Report of Alliance Defence Commission. Owen condemns Report as a 'fudge'.

1986	Sept.	SDP Council held at Harrogate.
		Liberals opt for unilateralism at Eastbourne Assembly.
1987	Jan.	Relaunch of Alliance at Barbican, London.
	26 Feb.	Rosie Barnes wins Greenwich for SDP in by-election.
	2 Mar.	Former SDP MP John Horam announces defection to Conservative Party.
	May	Alliance election manifesto, *Britain United*.
	11 June	General Election – SDP only five MPs.
	12 June	David Steel urges merger.
	6 Aug.	Ballot result of SDP members has majority in favour of opening merger talks. David Owen resigns as leader.
	29 Aug.	Robert MacLennan caretaker leader.
	31 Aug.	Portsmouth Council meeting votes for merger talks with Liberals.
	Sept.	Campaign for Social Democracy established.
1988	30–31 Jan.	Final Council meets in Sheffield and approves merger package by 273 votes to 28 against and 49 abstentions.
	2 Mar.	SDP membership ballot to approve merger declared with 65.3 per cent in favour and 34.7 per cent against.
	3 Mar.	Social and Liberal Democratic Party formally launched.
	8 Mar.	Dr Owen relaunches the SDP, with himself as leader and John Cartwright as President.
	14 July	Kensington by-election. SLD and SDP field candidates against each other.
	28 July	Paddy Ashdown elected leader of the SLD in a ballot of the membership by 41,401 votes (71.9 per cent) to 16,202 (28.1 per cent) for his rival candidate, former Deputy Leader of the Liberal Party, Alan Beith. Ian Wrigglesworth (the former SDP MP) elected President of the party.
	Sept.	SLD's first Conference adopts the term 'Democrats' as Party's short title.
	Nov.	Tawney Society disbands itself.
1989	Feb.	Paddy Ashdown launches discussion document 'Our Different Vision'.
	4 May	SLD net loss of 112 seats in County Council elections.
	June	Elections to the European Parliament. SLD receives only 6.23 per cent of the vote, and the SDP receives 0.48 per cent. The Greens, however, receive 14.52 per cent.

5

The Left Since 1964

JOHN CALLAGHAN

The growth of new radical issues and organisations can be traced back to the sixties when disenchantment with the Labour governments of Harold Wilson contributed to the loss of as many as 250,000 individual members of the party. Labour's abused and neglected activist base rebelled against Wilson's support for the American war in Vietnam, the proposal to sell arms to South Africa, and the racist Commonwealth Immigration Act of 1965. The government also alienated and angered many of the trade union leaders by pursuing policies of wage restraint and threatening to reorganise industrial relations along American lines by pressing ahead with the proposals contained in Barbara Castle's *In Place of Strife*. Even the party's moderates were forced to concede that the Wilson years had shown 'very little sign of a coherent, overall, egalitarian strategy' (Crosland, *Socialism Now*, 1974, p. 21). Economic performance had been disappointing and by 1970 and Labour's defeat in the general election there was no doubt that 'extreme class inequalities remain, poverty is far from eliminated, the economy is in a state of semi-permanent crisis and inflation is rampant' (ibid, p. 26).

But alongside this largely negative experience the sixties also saw the emergence of a revitalised and innovative left politics outside the Labour Party inspired by a variety of international developments – from the American civil rights movement to the events of May 1968 in Paris – and informed by a similarly eclectic range of theories associated with the names of Herbert Marcuse, Franz Fanon, R. D. Laing, Regis Debray and other heretical radicals. From this flux a new kaleidoscope of extra-parliamentary politics developed which included the women's liberation movement, student radicalism, a stress on direct action and community politics and a general critique of the established parties of the left (including the sclerotic Communist Parties). Into the left milieu which was created outside of the Labour Party stepped a number of Trotskyist organisations convinced that the time was ripe for open party-building. Now that Labour was seen as irrelevant, so too was the tactic of 'entryism' – infiltration of the larger party's organisations. In 1964 the Socialist Labour League (SLL) renounced entryism, followed by the International Socialists (IS) in 1965 and the International Marxist Group (IMG) in 1969. These groups now vied with the Communist Party for the title of revolutionary vanguard, though none of them even approached its industrial strength and 33,000 members. Only the little known Militant tendency – which had started life in 1957 as the Revolutionary Socialist League – preferred to remain buried within Labour's ranks; and the other Trotskyist groups were inclined to attribute this preference to Militant's ideological sterility. All the other groups believed that the auguries spoke of the feasibility of a British Leninist Party to be created from the militant shop stewards, rebellious students and feminists who now made the traditional concerns and style of Labourism seem painfully obsolescent. In 1973 the SLL became the Workers' Revolutionary Party (WRP); at the start of 1977 the IS became the Socialist Workers' Party (SWP); while the IMG sought to construct a British Section of Trotsky's Fourth International.

None of these projects was able to get beyond four-to-five thousand members and the declining Communist Party – itself caught in a clumsy transition from Stalinism to Eurocommunism – remained the biggest single Marxist organisation (current membership, approximately nine thousand). Nevertheless, tens of thousands of activists passed through these organisations and hundreds of thousands came into contact with them through such campaigns as Vietnamese Solidarity, the Anti-Nazi League, Rock Against Racism, the Troops Out Movement and the revived CND.

Then, as now, the revolutionary organisations exhibited very high annual membership turnovers (as high as 50 per cent). To those so inducted into left politics must also be added the militants attracted to the new feminism; the various environmentalist groups; the radicals involved in community politics such as the tenants', squatters', and claimants' organisations of the late sixties/ early seventies; the anti-racist groups, the solidarity campaigns, the peace movement, and so on. Many of these radicals returned individually to the Labour Party in search of a better vehicle for social change when the Leninist vanguard failed to materialise. Hopes for a socialist Labour Party were again raised on the left after 1970 when the party reacted against the failures of the Wilson years by bringing public ownership proposals back onto the immediate agenda. But as the move to the left in the Labour Party unfolded grassroots activists found themselves returning to constituency and ward organisations depleted in membership and devoid of political life. In the big cities in particular a variety of circumstances had turned the Labour strongholds into modern rotten boroughs in which a handful of activists and officials dominated the party organisations as if they were private fiefdoms. These were perfect for takeover by younger, more vigorous and less deferential recruits, many of whom had cut their teeth in the campaigns of the far left.

The legacy of 1964–70

The local election results of 1967 and 1968 which devastated Labour's council showing destroyed many of the power bases of the old Labourism in the big cities and opened the way for the younger generation when the electoral pendulum swung back to the party in the early seventies. By then its mass organisations had moved to the left in reaction to the disappointments of 1964–70. The unions in particular could no longer be relied upon to support the parliamentary leadership. Militant was a minor beneficiary of this trend. From 1970 it was able to dominate the Labour Party Young Socialists and in the absence of other entryists was the best organised faction in the National Organisation of Labour Students which it briefly captured in 1974. On Merseyside, Militant's long-standing infiltration of the local organisations – begun in the

Walton constituency in the 1950s – began to pay off in the form of a significant presence in Liverpool's Labour Group. But Militant was notably absent as an influence in those cities where an innovative left began to emerge, as in Sheffield, Manchester and London. Nor was Militant involved in the Campaign for Labour Party Democracy (CLPD) which was set up in 1973 in order to promote constitutional changes that would give the mass organisations more control over the parliamentary party.

However, Militant's demand that Labour should nationalise the '200 top monopolies' was no longer quite so marginal as it used to be. *Labour's Programme 1973* argued that the leading financial institutions and twenty-five major companies should be brought under state control in order to facilitate a 'fundamental and irreversible shift in the balance of power, and wealth . . . [to] . . . working people and their families'. These policies were never taken seriously by the Wilson and Callaghan governments after 1974, but they do indicate that mainstream party discourse was on the same state ownership wavelength as that of Militant. When the Labour Co-ordinating Committee (LCC) was set up by Michael Meacher and Frances Morrell in 1978 it was in order to campaign for the radical economic programme known as the Alternative Economic Strategy (AES) – variants of which were common currency on the Communist and Labour left, as well as to turn the Labour Party into a mass campaigning organisation. Within the parliamentary leadership Tony Benn was most closely associated with the developing left critique of Britain's political institutions and the promotion of a programme of participatory democracy designed to open these institutions to mass reforming pressures, while Stuart Holland did much to bring state ownership proposals back on to the Labour political agenda. Some of these ideas informed *Labour's Programme 1973* though Harold Wilson's personal veto prevented the specific demand to nationalise the biggest twenty-five companies – which had dominated the party's conference in 1973 – from entering the 1974 manifesto.

This intervention further fuelled demands to democratise the party's structures but did nothing to prevent the growth in support for the AES. By the end of the decade the party was committed to state-led industrial modernisation behind a protective shield of import controls and a programme of massive public expenditure. Among the factors which consolidated the rise of the left one would certainly have to include the perceived betrayal of the 1974 manifesto commitments, the deflationary budgets of 1976 and 1977 at the behest of the International Monetary Fund, the growth in unemployment and inflation, and the disastrous conflict with public sector unions as the government's fourth pay code foundered in the Winter of Discontent of 1978–9. But it is also worth pointing out that the parliamentary leadership of the party was unsympathetic to the growing demand for changes in Labour's constitution which would give greater power to the constituencies and the unions. This was given vivid demonstration when Newham North East constituency attempted to deselect Reg Prentice against the wishes of the party leadership in an affair which dragged on through 1975 and 1976; Prentice's subsequent defection to the Conservative Party only served to strengthen the argument that the parliamentary party was an obstacle to those among the grassroots who were fighting for the implementation of socialist policies – even though the parliamentary left was bigger than ever before with 86 members of the Tribune Group by 1978. Even within the left of the parliamentary party the old-style politics of the Tribune Group which had rarely questioned Labour's traditional paternalism and satisfaction with the institutions of government was under challenge. The Labour Co-ordinating Committee wanted to change the organisation into a mass campaigning force precisely because it doubted the efficacy of relying on purely parliamentary action for the achievement of socialism. According to the LCC:

> Britain is not as democratic a country as is often assumed. Our society is dominated by the class system; it has a ruling class who run financial and big business enterprises, the civil service, and the media. They have common interests in keeping elected government weak so that it does not interfere in their financial and industrial operations. So we must redistribute power as well as wealth and income.
>
> (Quoted by Seyd, 1987, p. 93)

Tony Benn had also referred to the need to look 'beyond parliamentary democracy' as early as 1970 but by the end of the decade the quasi-Marxist language of the LCC was proof that a significant change in the Labour left had occurred along the lines he had then anticipated. There was now much greater awareness of the need to reform state institutions and to attack irresponsible power wherever it lay – from the Labour Party itself to multinational corporations and the EEC. The promise of more participatory democracy which these arguments held out undoubtedly attracted radicals who wanted open government, greater powers for local government, a genuinely pluralistic socialism based upon the self-activity of working people, industrial democracy and the devolution of power generally. But insofar as this emphasis on extra-parliamentary action promised a greater reliance on class struggle and opportunities for would-be Leninist vanguards it also attracted a number of Trotskyist organisations back into the Labour Party and helped to give the Militant tendency greater plausibility and publicity. None of these groups were particularly devoted to open, pluralistic politics and for some of them the issues raised by other groups within the Bennite coalition – women, peace campaigners, Black Sections and so on – were frankly irrelevant or, worse, distractions from the class struggle. There was, then, considerable tension within this more amorphous Labour left between the populist and statist elements of the left's programme and constituency.

Re-groupings in the early eighties

The coalition of groups and interests which Benn sought to lead ranged from Militant, with its demand for a virtual command economy, to those principally concerned to devolve power within the party, the British state and society. In 1980 all these forces were brought together within the Rank and File Mobilising Committee. The success of Mrs Thatcher in the 1979 election strengthened the party's radical convictions and by a sort of demonstration effect reinforced the claims that a vigorous prosecution of class politics would sweep Labour to power. Benn gave effective voice to both the populist and statist currents of party opinion and in so doing attracted the attention of groups such as the Workers' Socialist League, the International-Communist League, and the International Marxist Group which returned to entryism as the campaign for constitutional reforms gathered momentum in 1978–9. These Trotskyist groups supported the new emphasis on exta-parliamentary action which had always been alien to the old Tribunite left and perceived the implementation of the AES as the first (inadequate) stage in the transition to socialism. The IMG now styled itself the Socialist League and changed its newspaper to *Socialist Action*. Other pro-Benn Trotskyists canvassed *Socialist Organiser* and of course *Militant*. In 1980 *London Labour Briefing* was established by others from the Trotskyist tradition but this soon became the organiser of the entire archipelago of left organisations in the city with the exception of die-hard sectarians like Militant. Similar initiatives were taken in Manchester and Birmingham and other cities. Specifically Trotskyist and other Leninist organisations, however, were always a minority trend within the Benn coalition and never held the initiative in either the CLPD or the LCC. Nevertheless, the new emphasis on direct democracy and direct action distinguished most interests in the left coalition from the rather paternalistic parliamentarism which had always characterised the radicalism of *Tribune*. Benn was never entirely popular with the Tribune Group of MPs and his decision to contest the deputy leadership of the party shortly after joining them in 1981 provided an opportunity for some of the old 'soft left' – notably Neil Kinnock and John Silkin – to express their dissent by abstaining in the vote and thereby allowing Denis Healey, a stalwart of the party right, to win by the slenderest of margins. Henceforward the Labour left was openly divided but the catalogue of destruction associated with Mrs Thatcher's first term of office helped it to retain confidence in the economic policies associated with the AES – including withdrawal from the EEC, state ownership of sections of industry, planning agreements, import controls, a large programme of public expenditure, steeply progressive taxation, and a commitment to reduce unemployment by two million within five years. The party also stood for unilateral nuclear disarmament and the removal of all US nuclear missiles from Britain. Buoyed up by the prospect of reversing the trends in the class struggle established by the Thatcher government few on the left envisaged any electoral problems with this programme of reforms. Only the Eurocommunist faction of the CP argued that the roots of Thatcherism had deep cultural sources which had been nurtured in part by the bureaucratic defects of the old social democratic consensus with which the left was still tainted. If the perceived defects of this tradition were problems of uniformity, stagnation, compulsion and state bureaucracy, what were the prospects of the left shaking off this unpopular legacy if it proposed to win power on the policies of the AES? Such an analysis of course cast serious doubts on the compatibility of the 1983 manifesto with the left's democratic and libertarian aspirations. But only the Eurocommunist journal *Marxism Today* consistently hinted at this conclusion.

Within the Communist Party a number of factions emerged in the early eighties appalled by the revisionist leanings of *Marxism Today*. From the summer of 1982 the party's daily newspaper, the *Morning Star,* openly declared war on the Eurocommunist element which seemed prepared to jettison the whole Leninist legacy of the party. Apart from the *Morning Star,* other defenders of the faith inside the CP were organised by *The Leninist* and *Straight Left.* All of these opposition groups maintained that Thatcherism was merely a typical form of Conservative reaction and as such required no major rethink of socialist policy.

Well before the general election of 1983, when the Bennite programme was subjected to a crushing defeat, the divisions within the Labour left had deepened into a permanent internecine war. Michael Foot, elected leader in November 1980, was the principal representative of the old *Tribune* left which prided itself on putting party unity before considerations of ideological struggle and which believed in the sanctity of parliamentary politics. Yet he inherited a situation which led, within months of his elevation to the leadership, to the departure of twenty-eight Labour MPs bound for a new Social Democratic Party accompanied by much media talk – encouraged by these same defectors – to the effect that the party had been taken over by extremists. Within months of this trauma the party was then plunged into a deputy leadership contest which lasted from April to October 1981. Foot publicly opposed the candidature of Tony Benn and came under tremendous pressure to stem the tide of radicalism which threatened to lead to more splits from the right of the party. The obvious target was Militant, whose four thousand or so members constituted the best publicised group of Marxists within the party and the only real evidence, drawn from the entryist origins of the group in the fifties, that the party was being taken over by alien elements at loggerheads with its commitment to parliamentary democracy. Foot accordingly gave the go-ahead to an inquiry into Militant's activities which resulted in the Hayward–Hughes Report of 1982 and the establishment of a register of all non-affiliated organisations within the Labour Party from which Militant could be excluded on the grounds of its status as a party with objects of its own. The subsequent expulsion of five members of the *Militant* editorial board and the endorsement of Foot's opposition to Militant by the party conference caused divisions within the CLPD, which had always campaigned for the observance of conference decisions, and further embittered relations within the Tribune Group; those who opposed the purge of Militant, led by Tony Benn, set up a separate Campaign Group of MPs (twenty-three in number) in December 1982. Meanwhile Foot's determination to rid the party of revolutionaries reached bathetic proportions when he declared that the party Executive would never endorse the candidature of Peter Tatchell, the Labour choice for Bermondsey who had talked about the need for 'extra-parliamentary' action to supplement the work of a Labour government. In the event Tatchell's candidature stood and Foot, who seems initially to have thought that he was fighting yet another entryist, was forced to recognise his error. This simply demonstrated that the 'hard left' whom Foot opposed was by no means confined to the tiny entryist groups in the party and in May 1982 even *Tribune,* which the Labour leader had himself edited for many years, became an organ of the Bennites when Chris Mullin became editor. Once again an inordinate row ensued with members of the 'soft left' led by John Silkin charging that *Tribune* was the victim of a coup and threatening legal action to restore it to its former cautious self.

Deepening divisions since 1983

The defeat of the Labour Party in the general election of 1983 deepened these divisions on the left. The manifesto on which Labour fought the election was by common consent as radical as any of the past. The government's record was unanimously held to be disastrous for the working class. Yet Labour's defeat was the worst it had suffered for over 50 years. It was now that the Bennite coalition collapsed as groups such as the Labour Co-ordinating Committee (LCC) joined forces with *Marxism Today* and Neil Kinnock's supporters to press for a policy rethink. Former Benn supporters such as David Blunkett and Michael Meacher had now regrouped into a larger soft left, conscious that the left had to put its own house in order before it could effectively take on Thatcherism.

The differences of style and strategy which divide the left can be illustrated by looking at the experience of the new local socialism which emerged in the early eighties. By 1982 socialist councils existed in Manchester, Sheffield, Stirling, Walsall, South Yorkshire and Merseyside as well as in half a dozen London boroughs, the GLC, and the ILEA. Some of these were centres of innovation in so far as they consciously set out to reorganise the political agenda in favour of the politics of the new social movements from which many of the councillors had themselves originated. Thus not only did they give a new priority to feminism, anti-racism, environmentalism and community politics, some of these councils also went to considerable lengths to create committees and monitoring groups composed of activists drawn from these movements. The GLC in particular used council resources to empower local organisations to promote their own concerns. In the financial year 1984–5, for example, the GLC dispensed £47m in aid to over one thousand community organisations. Before long the Press had invented a new political phenomenon – the 'looney left' – to describe the municipal socialists with their nuclear-free zones and apparently alarming disposition to fund unpopular pressure groups. But in Liverpool, where Militant was represented by sixteen of fifty-one Labour councillors from 1983, the activities of Ken Livingstone's GLC were regarded as mere *épater les bourgeois* (to shock the bourgeois) and a distraction from the real issues of job creation and new housing. Here Militant did its best to centralise power in its own hands by careful caucusing and control of the district Labour Party together with some of the local public sector unions. The idea of using council resources to encourage the self-activity of radical groups beyond its control was anathema to Militant as were the 'trendy middle-class' organisations which the GLC patronised. Instead everything was focused on an Urban Regeneration Strategy; if issues such as racism were to receive any independent attention they were to be dealt with on Militant's terms – such as by appointing a Militant supporter to the position of principal race relations advisor (to the fury of Liverpool's black organisations). Furthermore the council's plans were to be implemented without setting a legal rate and in defiance of the government's rate-capping policy. Sixteen other

Labour councils also refused to set a legal rate in 1985 but only the Liverpool group persisted with a course of open confrontation with the government and in September 1985 it was forced to announce 31,000 impending redundancies consequent upon the city's bankruptcy. At this point the council met with determined opposition from the unions as it became clear that the Urban Regeneration Strategy was being put before jobs and services. These events then led to the fiasco of an eleventh-hour loan of £30m raised from Swiss bankers and the scene was set for a Labour enquiry into Militant's power on Merseyside. The fact that leading members of Militant were subsequently expelled from the Labour Party without this leading to a united left campaign against 'the witch-hunt' is testimony to the rancorous sectarianism with which Militant always regarded other socialists and to the extent to which many of these were now totally estranged from it. But the Militant policy on Merseyside also demonstrated the limitations and embarrassing contradictions which a crude policy of centrally-manipulated confrontation was subject to and strengthened the position of Labour's revisionists.

Those who refused to countenance revisions of socialist fundamentals – especially concerning the need for extensive public ownership and solidarity with all elements engaged in confrontation with the government – regrouped with the hard left under the parliamentary leadership of Benn's Campaign Group. They are now supported by an unlikely combination of Trotskyist groups, such as Militant, *Socialist Organiser* and the Socialist League, and former factions of the Communist Party. In 1986 the hard left coalesced in the Labour Left Liaison which included the groups already mentioned together with the Labour Party Black Sections, the CLPD, Labour CND, the Labour Campaign for Lesbian and Gay Rights, the Labour Committee on Ireland, and the Labour Women's Action Committee. As this list demonstrates, the left's realignments have brought strange bedfellows together. Clearly the calculation is that whatever else may separate them ideologically all these groups suspect that the Labour leadership's rethink of socialist policy imperils principles which they share – if only the determination not to water down the causes for which they stand. As far as the otherwise warring Marxist groups are concerned some degree of co-operation has been made possible by a shared conviction that the manual working class remains by far the chief agency of socialist transformation. But this is a view which they see as under attack from both the Labour and Communist leaderships.

By January 1985 the Eurocommunists joined with the party's leading officials to purge the organisation of 'Stalinists'. Most of these fundamentalists – who believe that the CP has effectively abandoned the class struggle – regrouped as the Communist Campaign Group which retained control of the *Morning Star* and the People's Press Printing Society which has always owned it. Other groups of ex-CPers are organised by *The Leninist* and *Straight Left*. Most of the expelled membership initially believed that they could regain control of 'their' party, and certainly the CP is a much depleted force because of the purges of 1985–6. For the first time since the war the Communist Party now has virtually no industrial strength; youth membership has totally collapsed and the Young Communist League has folded up. 'Robbed' of its daily newspaper the party was forced to launch *Focus* (now *Seven Days*) on a weekly basis and be content with a circulation confined to party members.

Ten years ago it was possible for the Communist Party to organise its industrial support in briefing sessions prior to the Trade Union Congress and directly caucus about fifty delegates or 5 per cent of those at the TUC. In so doing the party provided a much bigger trade union left with a coherent line which focused and organised opposition within the movement. But this is no longer possible. Communist influence has decayed as the old centres of heavy industry have decayed and as the old rallying points and ideological certainties gave way before the present ideological disorientation. When the Communist Campaign Group announced in April 1988 that a new Communist Party of Britain (membership 1,500) had been formed – thus bringing to three the number of Communist Parties where once there had been a single monolithic organisation (if we include the declining New Communist Party which broke away in the mid-seventies) – this only formalised the irreconcilable ideological divisions within the old Stalinist left. Indeed so far has the CPGB moved away from the Leninist-Stalinist tradition that its latest attempt to modernise the *British Road to Socialism* (first adopted in 1951) has been applauded by Labour's leading revisionist Bryan Gould who only lamented that his own party could not so effectively free itself from the dead hand of the past. For the Eurocommunists have begun the revision of the party programme by publishing *Facing Up to the Future* (August 1988) which refers to the 'recomposition' of the working class, the 'contradictory class locations' which considerably complicate political allegiances, and rival organising principles of political action which challenge the centrality of class in the Marxist scheme of things. The Communist rethink also extends to public ownership, nuclear disarmament, the EEC, and the profound changes in the international economy and the structure of industry which have created new problems for the socialist movement. On all these issues the CPGB has not been afraid of heresy; indeed, the political editor of the *Sunday Times* was so impressed by the CP's mini-perestroika that he advocated lifting the ban on Communist membership of the Labour Party so that it could 'help [Kinnock] to turn outwards as they have. Doctrinally they are as pragmatic as he is. Organisationally they could take on both the hard left and the union stick-in-the-muds' (*Sunday Times*, 28 August 1988).

Policy and fragmentation in the late eighties

The Labour Party itself has been committed to a major policy review since its defeat in the 1987 general election and within a year was able to conclude the first phase of this process with the publication of a *Statement of Democratic Aims and Values* and *Social Justice and Economic Efficiency*. Here the party reaffirmed its commitment to the idea of positive freedom (where rights have meaning because people possess the economic and other means to realise them) and acknowledged that this entailed a large role for the state and public ownership, although the documents attempt to distinguish between the 'intrusive state' (which is rejected) and a pleasant-sounding 'enabling state'. It is impossible to know as yet what these documents will mean for Labour policy though it is already evident that the party leadership has retreated from unilateral nuclear disarmament and the traditional Morrisonian model of public ownership. Both documents reveal the extent to which Thatcherism has constructed the dominant political agenda in Britain even though neither attempts to analyse this experience or consider its sources in the contradictions of the old social democratic consensus. Absent too is any vision of the future and the policy review has been similarly vacuous on Labour's political goals. Instead the documents betray the fear that unless Labour can champion the values which the Conservatives have made their own the game is lost. It is presumably also from fear of electoral unpopularity that the party is specifically committed to tax relief on mortgages and rejects major political reforms such as a Bill of Rights, abolition of the House of Lords, and reform of the electoral system. Needless to say the policy review has only confirmed the militants in their suspicion that the new revisionism is a compound of temporising and betrayal of socialist principle but even those persuaded of the need for radical rethinking can detect little sense of urgency and direction in the published documents. Nevertheless, the challenges to the party leadership in 1988 were soundly repulsed at the annual conference. The disarray of the Labour left was revealed by the crushing majorities which the deputy leader, Roy Hattersley, was able to muster in all sections of the electoral college: 78.35 per cent of the trade union vote, 60.35 per cent of the constituencies and 57.92 per cent of the MPs.

Of course, a number of organisations, while favouring the class rhetoric of the Labour hard left, have remained largely apart from the internecine struggles which have consumed its energies. The Socialist Workers' Party has consistently maintained that Labour is useless as a vehicle for socialism and seeks to build an alternative party free from loyalties to either capitalism or state capitalism (the condition, it alleges, of the USSR). From this quarter other groups have emerged, such as the Revolutionary Communist Group (with its strong base in the Westminster group of Anti-Apartheid) and the Revolutionary Communist Party. As the journals of these organisations make clear – *Fight Racism! Fight Imperialism!* and *The Next Step* respectively – the key issues on which the Leninist vanguard must lead the way are those of racism and imperialism. These groups are accordingly prominent in solidarity campaigns with the victims of racism and imperialism – from South Africa to Northern Ireland – and expect to construct a 'coalition of the dispossessed' in the British ghettos. Their rivals in this project include the International Spartacist Tendency, which makes a specialism of disrupting other organisations of the left, and the anarchist journal *Class War,* which preaches direct action, organises events such as the Stop the City demonstrations of March and September 1985 and is involved in the activities of the Animal Liberation Front.

The most recent additions to this leftish archipelago originate from the Workers' Revolutionary Party which disintegrated in October 1985 after its founder and authoritarian leader, Gerry Healy, was expelled for alleged sexual misconduct. Supported by Corin and Vanessa Redgrave, Healy launched the Marxist Party at the Riverside Studios, Hammersmith in August 1987, thus bringing to six the number of fragments surviving from the original WRP. One of these groups – the Communist Forum – was briefly close to *The Leninist,* the former faction paper of the Communist Party. By September 1988 no less than nine organisations had been born out of the collapse of the Healy group with the International Socialist League, the Internationalist Faction, and the International Communist Party the most recently added to the list. But splits are not confined to left organisations outside the Labour Party. Entryist groups have also suffered. Neither course of action – entryist or independent party-building – has lived up even remotely to expectations. Thus the Socialist Organiser Alliance (formed in 1981 from the fusion of the International Communist League and the Workers' Socialist League) broke down in 1984 after a wave of expulsions. The Socialist League also split in 1985 when members of the editorial board of *Socialist Action* left to set up *International.* This was not the end of the trouble inside the Socialist League because another faction departed to form the Communist League of Britain in 1988. In short, the far left is littered with the debris from the three or four Trotskyist groups which existed in the sixties. Given the high level of volatility which currently pertains both organisationally and ideologically on the left, further exotic permutations may be expected and the old distinctions – such as Trotskyism, Stalinism, and Eurocommunism – are likely to become unimportant. In the absence of any evidence that these groups can establish a stable independent base, however, there is every reason to think that they will fight out their differences within the Labour Party.

Bibliography

Callaghan, J. (1987) *The Far Left in British Politics,* Basil Blackwell.
Crosland, C. A. R. (1974) *Socialism Now,* Cape.
Seyd, P. (1987) *The Rise and Fall of the Labour Left,* Macmillan.

6

Party Ideologies Since 1945

ALAN RYAN

The topic of this chapter can cause several sorts of intellectual cramp. Much of the discomfort is induced by the notion of ideology. Definitions of ideology divide social theorists – not only Marxist social theorists, either – and they divide political movements; the Conservative Party has characteristically been anxious to avoid any suggestion that it has an ideology. Ian Gilmour is typical: Conservatism 'cannot be formulated in a series of propositions which can be aggregated into a creed. It is not an ideology or a doctrine' (1977, p. 121). Just this claim is dismissed by opponents as an ideological ploy of a subtle and therefore peculiarly obnoxious kind.

Non-ideological Britain

The public at large seems unable to understand what the term 'ideology' means, or might mean; and the sociological literature is all but unanimous in claiming that the public's political attitudes are 'non-ideological' and do not cluster round deeply held beliefs about the class war, the rights and wrongs of private property, the legitimacy of political intervention in matters of private morality or anything else. Middle-class activists, delegates to party conferences, academics and theoreticians cleave to something it is proper to call 'party ideologies' – but then they would, wouldn't they? Or, as a recent study of the Labour Party more politely makes plain, 'it is clear that the ideological structuring of attitudes only occurs to a significant extent amongst the Labour elite' (Whitely 1983, p. 50).

Yet the American, Sam Beer, thought the extraordinary thing about British politics was its ideological character; French commentators, too, have been intrigued by the phenomenon of political parties whose professions of faith were both distinct in themselves and gave the voter some idea of what the parties would actually do in office if ever they were elected. Not that this was necessarily a good thing:

> Britain suffered unduly compared with some other, more successful, countries from sharp and usually ideologically inspired changes in direction – enactments and repeals, nationalisations and denationalisations.
>
> (Jenkins 1987, p. 3)

Herbert Morrison is famous for the claim that 'socialism is what a Labour government does', but this agreeable uninterest in theoretical essences was never the rule among politicians; even the pragmatic Anthony Crosland took it for granted that if his *Future of Socialism* was to have any point, it was essential to start with a definition of socialism, even one so banal as his claim that socialism is 'about equality'. A concern for definitional purity is surely the mark of the obsessive ideologist (Crosland 1956, p. 100; Beer 1970, p. 234).

The conventional picture of the changing party ideologies at the outset of the period under review – and one I shall not quarrel with to any great extent – is somewhat as follows: by 1945, an unideological (where 'ideology' is understood in the narrow sense of commitment to a highly articulated political theory) socialism had captured public opinion; it was socialist in that it was taken for granted that some elements of nationalisation and central planning were essential weapons in the fight for full employment and increased productivity. It was not socialist in most of the senses associated with the name of Marx. Though my friends and I marched round the school playground singing, 'We'll make Sir Anthony Eden wear a Fifty Shilling suit, when the Red Revolution comes', and Ernie Bevin announced, 'We're the masters now', victory in the class war was not the foundation of socialism's acceptability. Hysterical Conservatives of the stamp of Evelyn Waugh told themselves they were living in a country under alien occupation, but no sensible person believed a word of it (Jenkins 1987, pp. 83–4). Labour presented itself as the party of planning, full employment and the Welfare State. The revolutionary dictatorship of the proletariat was conspicuously not mentioned and the withering away of the state was not on the agenda.

Conservative rethinking after 1945

So much was this the dominant ideological mood (where 'ideology' is understood in the broad sense of a loosely structured set of beliefs about and attitudes toward major political issues) that the Conservative Party was somewhat at a loss for an answer. *Laissez faire* and a fiercely competitive economy was not the flavour of the month: after a war which had only been winnable on the basis of centralised planning, there were few takers for von Hayek's view that planning is of its nature totalitarian. Churchill's attempts to depict his opponents as likely to bring the Gestapo to Britain had backfired during the election campaign of 1945, and in any case the Conservative Party had always defended existing forms of private property and traditional conceptions of individual freedom rather than the highly theoretical libertarianism which finally came into fashion 30 years later. It was not, and could not in 1945 afford to be, the party of unbridled capitalism (Pinto-Duschinsky 1970, p. 61).

Into this ideological vacuum plunged Rab Butler and the Conservative Research Department. It was apparent to Butler that a reaffirmation of the rights of property was no way to seize the hearts and minds of the electorate; nor was an excess of anti-socialist fervour. Churchill was still inclined to make his hearers' blood run cold by threatening them with the totalitarian implications of voting Labour, but he never seemed entirely serious himself, and if anybody else took him seriously, it was only the more fired up members of the audience at party conference. Churchill might, in any case, be happy to wave the anti-socialist flag, but he never forgot that in the Liberal government of 1905–10 he and Lloyd George had competed for the title of father of the Welfare State; and as the case of Leo Amery suggests, Tory imperialism – or that branch of Conservatism which owes allegiance to the Liberal imperialism of Joseph Chamberlain – is in principle a better friend to the Welfare State than to competitive individualism. The conventional view is that Butler saved Conservatism by stealing Labour's clothes. In fact, what Butler produced was ideologically perfectly distinct from socialism, and even more so from 'labourism'.

Butler's line was less 'Butskellite' than legend has it. His *Industrial Charter* accepted the need for planning, accepted that full employment was an overriding goal, but was distinctively Conservative in its emphases, *pace* Beer (1970, p. 316). Industrial consultation was not seen as a way of giving some of the power of owners and managers to the workers; it was intended to bring home to the workers that they and the capitalists shared common interests. However feeble the Labour commitment to socialism has seemed at times, the Labour outlook on industrial democracy stressed the transfer of *power*: it was this that was anathema to Conservatives – it smacked of the class-war vision of society they deplored.

Employee share holdings and profit-sharing schemes, the former nowadays a plank in Bryan Gould's updated socialism and the latter an element in Alliance hopes for reconciliation between bosses and their workers, were suggested by Butler's charter as a way of creating harmony, but also as a way of heading off nationalisation. Against Labour's enthusiasm for centralisation, control from Whitehall and public ownership, the Conservatives set decentralisation – the dispersal of ownership rather than its concentration – and an emphasis on freedom as much as on efficiency. It was agreed that the Bank of England, coal and the railways were nationalised for good, but otherwise private ownership ought to be preserved and where necessary reintroduced.

Butler had some trouble getting the Conservative conference to support all this, but no more than anyone might have expected from a party feeling aggrieved at the loss of office after the best part of 15 years and eager for a simple call to arms (Beer 1970, p. 314). That so little of it came to pass is not entirely easy to explain; perhaps the incoming government of 1951 felt that it had no mandate for large reforms; perhaps the sudden return of prosperity between 1952–5 made it seem that the Conservative Party could retain office for as long as the economy kept it up, and an ageing Churchill settled for a quiet life.

Ideological consensus and the competence factor

Where in all this are the other issues which divide radicals and anti-radicals – the Empire, defence, the treatment of criminal and sexual deviance? The answer appears to be that although one could safely assume that Labour politicians would wish to grant self-rule to the colonies, would wish to abolish capital punishment, and would wish to spend money on housing rather then tanks, while their Conservative opponents would incline the other way, these were not issues which divided the parties in the political arena. If there was ideological conflict, there was also a massive ideological agreement – above all on the fact that political competition was essentially about 'bread and butter' issues. Parties 'could not ignore the fact that the mass of the electorate was more directly concerned with the standard of living than with the abstract causes championed by small fringe groups at either end of the political spectrum' (Pinto-Duschinsky 1970, p. 76).

Other things being equal, the electorate quite liked the existence of the Empire; but other things were not equal, and if it cost too much money and risked the lives of British soldiers, it had better go. Capital punishment has always been an odd issue in that the electorate evinces strong opinions in favour of it but readily allows MPs to decide against it on conscientious grounds. On defence issues generally, no party can afford to announce a defeatist or sceptical stance; once more, voters allow MPs to make up their minds for themselves, but only so long as they accept that it is their job to make sure the country is defended.

In essence, then, the ideological battle had to be fought on the socialist/anti-socialist front; equality versus freedom, rational planning versus the dangers of totalitarian control, private affluence and public squalor versus high taxation and resulting resentment. What makes it impossible to characterise the story so neatly, however, is the other major dimension along which voters have always ranked political parties. This is 'competence'. And competence as it emerges in electoral competition is a terribly unfair dimension in that it does not really reflect the parties' skills, judged by some dispassionate and objective test, but luck and chicanery. An incumbent party going to the polls in the middle of a boom will always score high on the competence scale, whether or not it has done anything to create the prosperity from which it benefits; conversely, a party going to the polls in time of trouble is likely to be judged incompetent even if it suffers from nothing but sheer bad luck. British governments from 1955 to 1987 have been re-elected on the strength of falling commodity prices and the resulting boost in real incomes more often than on the strength of anything for which they could decently take credit.

Labour's rethinking after 1951

The fifties were the decade in which the tables were decisively turned. Gaitskell and the Labour Party faced the problem which the Tories had faced after 1945: either people had to vote Labour out of ideological conviction, or Labour had to wait until the Conservatives struck an economic reef of comparable size and savagery to the Korean War which so damaged Labour's electoral prospects in 1951. The ideological front presented awful problems. It could no longer plausibly be said that socialism was the *sine qua non* of economic survival; Butler had claimed to 'set the people free', and they were at least prospering in a way they never had before. The fifties growth rate of a little under 3 per cent was historically an all-time high for the British economy, even if pretty feeble by the standards of West Germany and Japan. International comparisons had not yet begun to make themselves felt, and even if they had, the British standard of living was still much higher than that of the rest of Europe (Oppenheimer 1970, p. 140).

Labour faced the first of the 'modernisation' crises with which it has been plagued ever since. It was in a sense true that these crises had always been latent. Much of Labour's support rested on a sense that 'our people' needed a well-disposed government which would sacrifice capital to labour rather than the other way about; supporters of this kind would not readily rally to a 'white heat of technology' programme which might envisage wider differentials for skilled workers and supervisors, dramatic changes in the nature of industry and the nature of the work available, and so on. One part of Labour Party thinking, exemplified by the Webbs, had always taken it for granted that large differentials would survive into socialism, in order to recruit and motivate talented managers; but the growth of general unionism, from whence were drawn the block votes on which Attlee and Gaitskell had relied in their battles with the left, had gone along with an assault on differentials and a policy of looking for large hourly-rate increases in pay.

Another part of Labour thinking, exemplified in Roy Jenkins's defence of the Welfare State as the great promoter of equality, was egalitarian; this was fine by the general unions, but it ran into trouble with the growing power of skilled workers who saw that in any general egalitarianism they would lose as much as they gained. It was becoming clearer, too, that a more carefully targeted egalitarianism, which would pick off only the largest undeserved and unearned incomes was exceedingly hard to practise; but to be the party of equality only made sense if it could be done. It was no wonder that Crosland made economic growth the be-all and end-all of Labour policy, for he saw that the one way in which it might all be fudged was by allowing everyone to do better than they had, but to ensure that out of a constantly growing cake some took slices which grew disproportionately fast, while some hung back.

Ideological consensus in the fifties

Whether the Conservative Party possessed an ideology at all during this period is open to question. A vague commitment to productivity and prosperity which is all that some commentators have detected (Pinto-Duschinsky 1970, p. 77) hardly qualifies as an articulate social and political theory. Beer saw the two parties as increasingly divided on 'questions of "more" or "less" rather than great social theories in conflict' and concluded that ideological issues were decreasingly at stake at all. Differences were 'marginal, statistical, quantitative' (Beer 1970, p. 242). Economic management, the maintenance of the Welfare State and the appeasement of pressure groups *à l'américaine* provided the rationale of political competition. Nobody denied that steady inflation-free growth was the great *desideratum;* competition was only permitted concerning the best way to achieve it and the competence of both front benches to implement the policies they advertised. In this competition, as everyone noted at the time,

Labour was handicapped by the existence of the 'deferential voter', alternatively characterised as the 'working-class Conservative', and the heir of the 'angels in marble' that Disraeli had perceived (McKenzie and Silver 1968). The working-class Tory just couldn't believe that the country could be governed by anything but a traditional ruling class. The Conservative Party enshrined the know-how of the natural aristocracy. Its competence was taken for granted; it had to lose its credit to lose an election, where Labour leaders had to gain it to win.

One under-commented-on aspect of this non-ideological political competition may deserve the appellation of an ideological prop to non-ideological politics. This was the Conservatives' attempt to wrap themselves in the mantle of Monarchy, Church and Military. Hailsham's *Case for Conservatism* wavered between suggesting that opponents of Conservatism were necessarily unChristian and hardly to be tolerated at all and, less objectionably, that decent opposition was permissible only within a Christian framework. The thought that the Church of England was the Conservative Party at prayer was not then the joke it has lately become. Given the Labour Party's base in Methodist and Nonconformist religious allegiances, it was an obvious piece of cheek to try to suggest that Conservatives were uniquely entitled to govern a Christian country, though there were innumerable distinctively Methodist Tories, too (Jenkins 1987, pp. 83–4). Still, when the Queen as head of state and defender of the faith was brought into the picture, it was less implausible to suggest that the Christian faith as by law established was something to which Conservatives were more naturally attached than were their rivals.

As for seizing the monarchy's glamour for party purposes, someone with the passion for history that Churchill possessed could hardly have been unaware of the similarities between his position vis-à-vis the new Queen and the position of Lord Melbourne vis-à-vis the young Victoria. It is not clear just how monarchist the British public actually is, but it certainly did Churchill's image as national leader no harm to present him as a sort of constitutional uncle to a new sovereign. The Conservatives had never hesitated to suggest that the symbols of national identity belonged to them and them alone, and they continued throughout the fifties to give the impression that Labour was inclined to atheism, republicanism and pacificism and that they alone could be trusted to keep Britain great.

The effect of the erosion of British economic advantage over the rest of Europe, the retreat from Empire, the defeat at Suez and recurrent small economic crises were in part to facilitate the rise of the Liberal Party. This had little impact on the ideological climate, and the Liberals had since 1929 become gloomily accustomed to seeing good ideas about policy pinched by their rivals; there was little in Butler's *Industrial Charter* that wasn't in prewar Liberal papers from the Yellow Book onward. The Liberal share of the vote had collapsed to 2–5 per cent from 1945 onward – the lowness of the figure reflecting the party's diminished capacity for fighting large numbers of seats at all as well as the fact that it could hardly expect to save its deposit in most of the seats it did fight.

At the end of the fifties it became clear that the two-party fight was largely a fraud: Labour did not intend to introduce Soviet-style socialism, and the Conservatives did not intend to exhume nineteenth century capitalism. Yet each painted the other in such terms, and the electorate began to wonder whether the sham battle wasn't a distraction from the real tasks of government. The Liberals could seize on the British liking for compromise, and the widespread dislike of notions of class war and adversarial politics generally; their desire for electoral reform appealed to the British ideals of fairness (Fulford 1959); and their Europeanism was at least felt to be up to date, even if most people found the EEC a turn-off. From 1958 and the Torrington by-election, the Liberals were increasingly able to capitalise on Tory mid-term disasters. The perceived taste for freedom, moderation and common sense which the Liberal Party embodied under Jo Grimond made it an attractive home for the protest vote, and perhaps more than that. By the end of the fifties it was commonly true that a near majority of the electorate said that they would have voted for the Liberals if they had had any chance of victory.

Ideological ferment on its left in the sixties

From 1960 onward the party battle was, ideologically speaking, more and more a three-way split – where it wasn't multi-dimensional as new varieties of dissident leftism came to the fore. So far as the production of ideological perspectives as such went, the sixties was a wonderfully fertile period – usefully described by John Callaghan in the previous chapter. The British New Left, founded in 1957, was the product of boredom with orthodox, 'apathetic' politics on the one hand, and the break-up of British communism after Hungary on the other. It made little headway during the late fifties, but by the mid-sixties something close to a fusion of dissident attitudes had taken place – not that one group or one issue ever swallowed up the whole non-parliamentary left, nor that an 'anti-system' coalition was in business. Nuclear disarmament, anti-racism, violent hostility to the American presence in Vietnam, feminism, a passion for intellectual revolution and a liberation from academic constraints in literature and the social sciences all coalesced – not in a political programme or a political movement so much as in a hostility to orthodox politics and to conventional assumptions about the content and method of that politics.

This posed organisational difficulties for the Labour Party, rather than intellectual or ideological ones. The Labour Party was too big and too solidly supported by trade unions interested in 'bread and butter' to go haring off after Herbert Marcuse or Bertrand Russell. As for the Conservatives, they could safely ignore the whole upsurge of feeling; from 1964–70 a Labour government was in power which felt the wrath of the disappointed idealists, and found its natural grip on the sympathies of the young voter much loosened by their defection to the 57 varieties of Trotskyism, post-Trotskyism and, towards the end of the decade, to such foreign importations as situationism. The main long-term recipients of the allegiance of the disaffected idealists seem to have been two, often loosely allied, groups: one, the Bennite radicals, whose ideas owed more to the Levellers and William Cobbett than to Karl Marx and Leon Trotsky (Benn 1981, p. 123ff); the other, the entryist Trotskyites of Militant. The main beneficiary has undoubtedly been Mrs Thatcher.

The *groupuscules* of the left would have been no more than a minor irritant had the Labour governments of the sixties been more successful than they turned out to be in modernising the economy. Although it was Hugh Gaitskell who had the clearest conception of what it needed to modernise the Labour Party itself, it was only under Harold Wilson that the party committed itself to a modernising ideology. The winning slogan of 1964, 'thirteen wasted years', expressed a technocratic and technological ideal which owed next to nothing to traditional concerns for 'our people' and almost everything to a vague idea that government-sponsored mergers and government-sponsored high-technology projects together with indicative planning would at last get Britain's economy moving and take the country out of the cycle of 'stop-go' which had marked the economic policy of the various Conservative governments since 1951 (Bogdanor 1970, pp. 104–6).

In putting forward this 'white heat of technology' line, the Labour Party was much assisted by the way in which Macmillan had overplayed his unflappable Edwardian style. What in good times had appeared to be a justified confidence in his own capacities and a nicely judged reassurance that he could be effective without being merely the ally of the grasping capitalist turned out in bad times to be an irritant (Siedentop 1970). The country's sense that too much in Britain was out of date and hopelessly inefficient was simply aggravated by his attempts to pretend that the country was never faced by anything worse than little local difficulties. Sir Alec Douglas-Home was, in public relations terms, a disastrous choice as Macmillan's successor in 1963; while in fact he very nearly managed to snatch victory at the 1964 general election, in appearance he suggested that the Conservatives were trying to govern from the grouse moor.

Quite what one ought to say about the ideological complexion of the 1964–70 Labour governments, it is hard to tell. Harold Wilson may have begun as the apostle of white heat technology, but he soon found himself struggling with the familiar British diseases of low growth, weak currency and a persistent tendency to run an inflation rate higher than our competitors'. Dick Crossman's fifties doctrine that the economic and technical successes of the Soviet Union would force socialism on the British was not seen to be entirely silly. The socialist countries might be able to put men into space but seemed incapable of putting food into Moscow shops. There was a curious divergence between the general sensation that there was lots of money about and that anyone could become well off if they wanted to, and the administrative and governmental difficulties of combining growth, full employment and low inflation. Pay policies, indicative planning, attempts to incorporate the unions in the determination of policy all came to nothing. The growth rate, always slower than that of the rest of Europe, got slower still.

Enter Heath: consensus attacked

It was at this point that the first major attack on consensus was launched by Edward Heath. He had always been sceptical of the existence of the famed consensus which his successor as leader of the Conservative Party was so memorably to attack. At the end of the Wilson government of 1964–70, he committed the party to a capitalist revival. The motto was to be 'stand on your own two feet' and the symbol of the ruthless pursuit of efficiency was to be the death of the lame duck. In so far as the Conservative Party has had an ideology at all, it had one at the time of 'Selsdon Man'. Whether Heath could have made the policy of 'no lame ducks' stick under any circumstances is an open question; he was an unexpected victor in the 1970 general election, and the taint of earlier losses clung to him. He had done nothing to prepare the ground for a successfully confrontational policy towards the unions and yet his cry of 'stand on your own feet' pretty well guaranteed non-cooperation from them.

Whether this was enough to inspire the curious outbreak of ideological enthusiasm from left and right which now occurred is mysterious. On the face of it, successful corporatism, more or less socialist as in Sweden or more or less capitalist as in West Germany, ought to have been the flavour of the epoch. Rational unionists should have been able to see that leap-frogging wage demands were no way to a secure improvement in living standards, and that while stronger groups might hope that when the music stopped they'd be holding the parcel, weaker groups knew they had little hope of that. Yet general workers showed as much hostility to Heath's post-'U-turn' attempts to incorporate them into a new social compact as did groups like the miners.

The post-1974 Labour Party did seem to understand the logic of the case. What the party was not much good at was frightening the union movement into compliance with policies everyone agreed to be sensible. Amid the raging inflation of 1974–6 the unions persisted in demanding wage increases which would keep their members ahead of inflation and price restraint, which would ensure that the employers had no resources with which to meet their demands. The Liberal Party, still some years away from the injection of support that it received at the end of the decade and during the early eighties, had nothing to offer except a refuge for those who thought that neither the Labour Party nor the Conservatives really had a clue about how to govern the country – a role it had played for years (Fulford 1959).

In a manner of speaking, the ideological conflict was less about the politics of the day than about how to get out of those politics altogether. The nostrum of the Bennite left was ultra-democracy: not a Marxist party dictatorship but something almost wholly untheoretical and populist. The right was less ideologically fluent than it has since become, but it was already beginning to see that one way out was to take the government out of the firing line. If governments did not try to plan, did not set wage norms, did not take responsibility for full employment, and did not suggest that the Welfare State could be protected against every economic storm that blew, government authority would be less at risk.

The replacement of Edward Heath by Margaret Thatcher in 1975 was not a move towards ideological coherence, nor was it a move away from consensus to conviction politics (Jenkins 1987, *passim*; Vincent 1987). This is a vision imposed by hindsight. Mrs Thatcher's politics are essentially eclectic, not ideological. The combination of nationalism with a blind faith in the market is in many ways incoherent, as is the combination of public moralising with assaults on the idea of the nannying welfare state. Nonetheless, they are an effective electoral package, appealing to much the same populist irration with establishment politics that Bennite ultra-democracy appeals to.

Ideological volatility since 1979

Since 1979 the situation, oddly, is hard to describe. The easy description is one in which the 'new right' is in the ascendant, the left fragmented into 'hard' and 'soft', and the Labour Party lost in a fog of anxiety about the redefinition of socialism. From Morrison's assertion that socialism is what the Labour Party does, we have moved to the queasy thought that socialism is what the party would do if only it could discover what it is. It is no longer a search for the Holy Grail but a hunt for a snark, the nature of the beast, and its location, being alike unknown – a fact all too apparent in Austin Mitchell's 1983 *Case for Labour*. Yet this is not primarily a matter of Labour losing an ideological battle or losing its way intellectually. It has of course been wracked by ideological conflict, but that is the effect of political failure rather than its cause. The electorate still cares next to nothing for ideological commitments, left or right. To the extent that principles agitate the electorate, they favour the Labour Party's 'compassionate' image and its commitment to the Welfare State; Mrs Thatcher's 'Iron Lady' image is respected but not loved, the Labour Party's nicer face loved but not respected.

What has wrecked the Labour Party is not ideological disunity – it has never possessed it. What has wrecked the Labour Party is its inability to stand up to the union movement and its inability to deliver even moderate economic growth. Mrs Thatcher's governments have a pretty spotty record on growth; the gains of the last couple of years have to be set against the first three years of self-inflicted slump, and rises in productivity have to be set against a diminution of the total physical product and the crippling of manufacturing industry. But it was always clear that the government intended to govern, and more crucially that it was not going to let anyone else do so. Even when Mrs Thatcher was forced to give ground to the miners in 1982, it was plain to everyone, save Arthur Scargill, that this was *reculer pour mieux sauter*. When one reflects on the appallingly ham-fisted way the government and the NCB fought their side of the miners' strike of 1984–5, it is apparent how broad and deep the current of dislike for the NUM was running in the country at large, and how much pleasure the electorate derived from its demolition. A nicer leader than Mrs Thatcher would have been able to capitalise on this dislike even more than she did – if she ever uttered a word of sympathy for the plight of miners' families or a word of appreciation for the courage with which the miners stuck to a cause which was visibly lost from the first day of the strike, nobody seems to have recorded it (Adeney and Lloyd 1986). Yet her victory answered the question which the seventies had raised: 'Is Britain governable?' The answer may well be 'at a rather high price', but it certainly isn't 'no'.

If it didn't conjure up so many inapt analogies one might say that the one piece of traditional Tory ideology which she pressed into service was the leadership principle. Groups which for twenty years made everyone's life a misery – the train drivers, the printers, the car workers and the miners, to mention but a few – have been seen off by sheer will power. Of course it is all quite preposterous: in a rational world, the modified corporatism of the Alliance would be the order of the day, and one would expect the TUC and the Labour Party to converge on something like the German model of *Mitbestimmung* (Beith 1983). Equally the Conservative Party would not be tempted by Hayekian delusions of a return to the free market of 1850 or thereabouts but would understand clearly that what it is doing in fact is running an economic system which actually needs continuous government tinkering to enable it to survive at all, and that it might as well start from there in formulating policy. But, so long as the Labour Party affects to believe that Clause Four socialism is still on, the Conservative Party can affect to believe that the country needs a strong leader to save it from the Reds and that what is being saved is free enterprise.

Bibliography

Adeney, M. and Lloyd, J. (1986) *The Miners' Strike, 1984–5,* Routledge.

Beer, S. (1970) *Modern British Politics,* Faber.

Beith, A. (1983) *The Case for the Liberal Party and the Alliance,* Longman.

Benn, A. (1981) *Arguments for Democracy,* Cape.

Bogdanor, V. and Skidelsky, R. (eds) (1970) *The Age of Affluence, 1951–1964,* Macmillan.

Bogdanor, V. (1970) 'The Labour Party in opposition, 1951–1964', in Bogdanor and Skidelsky (eds).

Callaghan, J. (1987) *The Far Left in British Politics,* Basil Blackwell.

Crosland, C. A. R. (1956) *The Future of Socialism,* Cape.

Fulford, R. (1959) *The Liberal Case,* Penguin.

Gilmour, I. (1977) *Inside Right,* Quartet.

Hailsham, Lord (1959) *The Case for Conservatism,* Penguin.

Hennessy, P. and Seldon, A. (1987) *Ruling Performance,* Basil Blackwell.

Jenkins, P. (1987) *The Thatcher Revolution,* Cape.

McKenzie, R. T. and Silver, A. (1968) *Angels in Marble,* Chicago University Press.

Mitchell, A. (1983) *The Case for Labour,* Longman.

Oppenheimer, P. (1970) 'Muddling through: the economy 1951–1964', in Bogdanor, V. and Skidelsky, R. (eds).

Pinto-Duschinsky, M. (1970) 'Bread and circuses?: the Conservatives in office, 1951–1964', in Bogdanor, V. and Skidelsky, R. (eds).

Siedentop, L. (1970) 'Mr Macmillan and the Edwardian style', in Bogdanor, V. and Skidelsky, R. (eds).

Vincent, J. (1987) 'The Thatcher Governments, 1979–83', in Hennessy, P. and Seldon, A. (eds).

Whitely, P. (1983) *The Labour Party in Crisis,* Methuen.

7

Funding of Political Parties Since 1945

MICHAEL PINTO-DUSCHINSKY

Sources of money

Ever since 1945, British party organisations have retained the same, distinctive pattern of fundraising. The Labour Party has been almost totally dependent for its national finances on the political levy funds collected by trade unions. Labour Head Office has derived 80–90 per cent of its income from the unions during most of the period. The unions have usually provided about 50–55 per cent of overall party income (including constituency and regional as well as national organisations). Gambling schemes have been the largest single source of constituency income.

The Conservatives have been able to draw on a wider variety of sources. Company contributions have normally supplied about 60 per cent of the party's central income and approximately 30 per cent of overall income (i.e. local and national combined). The fact that individual Conservative membership has been far larger than Labour's has given the party a vital additional source of money. The large number of small contributions raised by members of Conservative constituency associations, mainly through social events such as coffee mornings, jumble sales or wine and quiche receptions, have produced in total more than the money given by companies. The party has also continued to benefit centrally from some large and medium-sized individual contributions and bequests. The extent of these payments and the identity of the donors has remained a closely-guarded secret. Individual donations and bequests have probably accounted for a fifth of the income of Conservative Central Office during most of the period since 1945.

The effects of Labour's reliance on trade union payments and the somewhat lesser dependence of the Conservatives on company payments cannot scientifically be measured. According to one interpretation, a natural identity of interests and sympathies – not money – is the basis of the link between each of the main parties and its institutional sponsors. The connections would be as close, if this view is accepted, even if unions ceased to act as Labour's financial mainstay or if corporations reduced their payments to the Conservatives. As Keith Ewing has argued, '(i)t would be wrong to say that the Conservatives are pro-business simply because they are financed by business or that Labour is pro-union because that is where the bulk of its money comes from. The relationship is much more subtle than that' (*The Funding of Political Parties in Britain,* p. 177). Nevertheless the impact of political contributions should not be dismissed.

The pattern of party fundraising has at the very least reinforced the bonds of Conservative and Labour with rival business and employees' organisations. Indeed, it has probably been a significant influence on the development of party policies, for both practical and symbolic reasons. Corporate payments have underlined the status of the Conservatives as the party of business. More important, reliance on political levy funds has ensured that Labour has remained moored to the unions (even though a majority of individual trade unionists do not vote Labour in general elections). There is a direct connection between the affiliation fees paid by each union to Labour's National Executive Committee and the size of its block vote at the annual party conference. A union may add to its voting power simply by increasing its subscription, regardless of whether its membership has actually grown or not.

The pattern of institutional funding has been significant for another reason. It has given the two established parties an advantage over the smaller parties of the centre. The relative weakness of third party funding has been the consequence partly of their failure to secure regular access to institutional contributions and partly from their relatively low memberships.

When in power, each of the main parties has passed legislation to benefit its own income and to undermine that of its opponent. The Labour government's Trade Union Act, 1946, replaced 'contracting in' to trade union political levy funds by 'contracting out'. The number of union members contributing to political levy funds grew from 2.9 million in 1945 to 5.6 million in 1947. In 1967, another Labour government introduced a Companies Act, which obliged companies to disclose political contributions exceeding £50 (increased later to £200). In their turn, the Conservatives were responsible for the Trade Union Act, 1984, making it illegal for unions to raise political levies without balloting their members at least every ten years. (All unions holding ballots since 1984 have secured majorities in favour of retaining political levies. Moreover, several additional unions have voted to establish them. The legislation has therefore left Labour finances unharmed.)

The most significant recent trend concerning political contributions has been the success of the unions in increasing, in real terms, the income of their political levy funds despite the sharp drop in union membership and in the number contributing to political levies (5.5 million in 1986 compared with 8.1 million in 1979). Since the seventies, union payments to Labour Party politics have, in total, overtaken company contributions to the Conservative Party.

Though institutional payments to the two main parties are still the main sources of their incomes, they now seem to provide a somewhat smaller percentage of the total than before. In 1983–7, the trade unions supplied about three-quarters of Labour's central income while companies accounted for between two-fifths and a half of central Conservative income.

Another development has been the growth in fundraising by computerised, direct mail appeals to members and potential sympathisers. This method was successfully used by the Social Democratic Party after its foundation in 1981. For the two main parties, however, direct mail has so far provided only a small proportion of income (probably about 5 per cent of Conservative Central Office income in 1987).

Table 7.1 Trade union political levy funds, 1945–85

	No. contributing (millions)	Total income (£ million) current prices	At June 1987 prices (£ million)
1945	2.9	0.2	3.6
1950	5.8	0.5	6.1
1955	6.2	0.6	5.6
1960	6.4	0.8	6.9
1965	6.6	0.9	7.4
1970	6.7	1.1	6.7
1975	n.a.	2.3	7.1
1980	7.7	5.0	7.7
1985	5.7	10.0	10.8
1986	5.5	10.3	10.7

Note: Nearly 80 per cent of political fund income is paid immediately or after an interval to central, regional and local Labour Party organisations and to sponsored candidates. If payments for sending union delegates to party meetings are included, the proportion devoted to Labour Party purposes is about 87 per cent.

Source: Pinto-Duschinsky (1981), Table 58.

Comparison between the size of Conservative, Labour and Alliance Income

Throughout the postwar period, the Conservatives have been richer than Labour, but the party's advantage has been smaller than usually supposed and it has been declining. As far as national funds are concerned, the routine (that is, non-election) budget of Conservative Central Office was three times as great as Labour's until the sixties. By 1984–86, however, routine, national Conservative income was only 20 per cent greater than Labour's. This change resulted from the growth of trade union payments to Labour Head Office.

If election as well as routine income is taken into account, the Conservatives received some 40 per cent more than Labour in the 1983–7 parliamentary cycle. (For further details about Conservative versus Labour central income, see Pinto-Duschinsky (1981), especially pp. 277–8; Pinto-Duschinsky (1985), p. 335; and Pinto-Duschinsky (1989), footnote 7.)

In general election campaigns, Conservative parliamentary candidates have usually outspent Labour by some 10 per cent. (In 1945, Tory candidates spent 31 per cent more than their Labour

Table 7.2 Routine income of Conservative Central Office and Labour Head Office, 1947–86 (£ million)

	Conservative	June 1987 prices	Labour	June 1987 prices
1947	n.a.	n.a.	0.2	2.3
1951*	0.9	10.1	0.2	2.3
1954	0.6	6.3	0.2	1.9
1958	0.6	5.2	0.3	3.1
1961	0.6	5.2	0.3	2.2
1964*	1.1	8.9	0.3	2.1
1967	0.8	6.0	0.4	2.5
1970*	1.5	9.3	0.6	3.9
1972	1.2	6.2	0.7	3.6
1975	1.9	5.8	1.4	4.2
1978	2.4	4.9	1.9	3.9
1981	4.1	5.6	3.7	5.0
1983*	5.7	6.8	4.1	4.9
1985	5.0	5.4	4.9	5.3
1986	8.6	8.9	6.1	6.3
1987*	6.3	6.3	5.6	5.6

Note: Asterisks denote general election years. Routine income is defined as total income minus estimated general election spending. In much of the period, routine Conservative income has been highest in general election years.

Source: Pinto-Duschinsky (1981), Tables 28 and 38.

counterparts but only 5 per cent in 1964. There has been no trend.) At national level, the Conservatives spent over two-and-a-half times as much as Labour in the 1959 general election (the largest margin since the Second World War) and only one-fifth more than Labour in the 1970 general election.

The most distinctive Conservative funding advantage has derived from routine constituency income. In 1973, when Conservative membership totalled 1.2–1.5 million compared with Labour's 0.3 million, the Houghton Committee's survey showed that the income of an average Conservative constituency organisation (£4,713) was over two-and-a-half times greater than the Labour average (£1,804).

Absence of information (much of which appears to have been destroyed or lost) combined with the complexities of Liberal Party accounting preclude accurate comparisons between Liberal funds and those of the two main parties for the forties through to the sixties. In the seventies, the income of the national and regional organisations of the Liberal Party was about one-tenth of Conservative Central Office income. Liberal national-level spending on

Table 7.3 Conservative and Labour central expenditure on general election campaigns, 1951–87 (£ million)

	Conservative		Labour		Conservative
	At current prices	At June 1987 prices	At current prices	At June 1987 prices	Spending as % of Labour spending
1951	0.11	1.3	0.08	0.9	140
1955	0.14	1.4	0.07	0.7	195
1959	0.63	5.8	0.24	2.2	264
1964	1.23	9.9	0.54	4.3	229
1966	0.35?	2.6	0.20	1.4	178?
1970	0.63	3.8	0.53	3.2	120
1974 (Feb.)	0.68	2.7	0.44	1.7	155
1974 (Oct.)	0.95	3.4	0.52	1.9	181
1979	2.33	4.3	1.57	2.9	149
1983	3.8	4.5	2.3	2.8	167
1987	9.0	9.0	4.7	4.7	192

Note: Includes estimated Labour regional spending in elections from 1979.
Source: Pinto-Duschinsky (1981), Tables 31 and 41 and, for 1983 and 1987, Conservative and Labour Party officials.

general elections varied between one-tenth of Conservative spending (in 1979) and one-fifth (in 1970 and February and October 1974). At constituency level, the Liberals were at less of a disadvantage. In 1973, average routine Liberal income (£964) was half of average Labour income and one-fifth of average Conservative income. In general elections, the cost of constituency campaigning inhibited the Liberal Party from putting forward a full slate of candidates until 1974. In the two 1974 campaigns, the average expenses of Liberal candidates were over half those of Conservative candidates and in 1979 slightly under half.

Following the foundation of the Social Democratic Party, the new Liberal–SDP Alliance significantly improved its finances as compared with those of the Liberal Party in the seventies. In particular, the SDP's central fundraising proved more effective than that of the Liberals. In 1981, the combined routine national funds of the two Alliance Parties were nearly a quarter the size of Conservative funds. In the 1983 general election, national Alliance spending (including grants to constituencies) was six times greater in real terms than Liberal spending in 1979 and was half as great as central Conservative campaign spending. In constituency campaigns, too, Alliance candidates caught up and spent three-quarters as much as Conservative candidates both in 1983 and 1987.

A comparison between the incomes of the different party organisations needs also to take account of the value of the subsidies in kind which they receive. All parliamentary candidates receive free use of halls for election meetings and the free postage of an item of mail to each elector. In addition, free time for television and radio broadcasts is provided for all the major parties between elections and during campaigns. The effect of these subsidies is greatly to reduce the financial gap between the parties. In each general election campaign since 1970, the Conservative and Labour parties have each been allotted fifty minutes of free time on all television channels, and the Liberals (or Alliance) have received thirty minutes in 1970, February 1974 and 1979, forty minutes in October 1974 and 1983 and fifty minutes in 1987. In the 1987 general election campaign, the estimated value of subsidies-in-kind totalled £13.2m each for Conservative, Labour and Alliance parties. This compared with total election expenditure (central and local) of £11.7m by the Conservatives, £6.5m by Labour and £3.2–3.4m by the Alliance.

Patterns and trends of political expenditure

Although attention is usually focused on the cost of election campaigns, the bulk of party political expenditure since 1945 has been devoted to the routine maintenance of national and constituency organisations between elections. In the parliamentary cycle 1983–7 for example, routine spending by the Conservative, Labour and Alliance parties was over six times greater than their combined spending on the 1987 general election.

Another feature of British party funding is the importance of local as opposed to central spending. As will be suggested later, central party spending seems to have been catching up with constituency spending. However, the total spent locally by Conservative, Labour and Alliance parties is probably still greater than spending by the central organisations. This includes routine as well as campaign spending. If campaign spending alone is considered, the party organisations now spend more at the centre than at constituency level. For example, in the 1987 general election, spending by parliamentary candidates of the major parties amounted to £7.5m, while the national and regional

Table 7.4 Proportion of overall political spending devoted to routine versus campaign costs and devoted to central versus constituency spending (in per cent)

	Conservative (parliamentary cycle 1966–70)	Labour (parliamentary cycle 1970–74)	Liberal (parliamentary cycle 1970–74)
Central			
Routine	30.8	39.2	22.2
Campaign	4.5	4.2	2.8
Total	35.3	43.4	25.0
Constituency			
Routine	60.6	47.2	60.7
Campaign	4.1	9.3	14.3
Total	64.7	56.5	75.0
Routine – total	91.4	86.5	82.9
Campaign – total	8.6	13.5	17.1
Total	100.0	100.0	100.0

Source: Pinto-Duschinsky (1981), Appendix D.

Conservative, Labour and Alliance organisations spent £14m (excluding grants to candidates).

The only type of political expenditure limited by the Representative of the People Act is that of parliamentary candidates. Election spending by national party organisations and routine spending, local and national, is not controlled. In the 1983–7 parliamentary cycle, spending by parliamentary candidates constituted only 5 per cent of overall local and central, routine and campaign expenditure. Despite the fact that 95 per cent of party spending is not subject to a legal ceiling, there has been no escalation of political costs in the period since 1945. This will be seen by examining constituency (routine), national (routine), constituency (campaign), and national (campaign) categories.

Constituency (routine) spending

Routine constituency budgets have not regularly been collected and analysed by the national party organisations. It is, therefore, not possible to give accurate statistics of trends. However, there is considerable evidence that constituency finances have declined since the sixties. In both the Conservative and Labour Parties, membership peaked in the fifties. Labour membership dropped from 1.0 million in 1952 to 0.3 million by 1970. Conservative membership reached its all-time high of 2.8 million in 1953 and has subsequently fallen to little over 1 million. Falling membership appears to have been accompanied by financial decline. Estimates of Conservative constituency income in 1966/7 and 1977/8 indicated a decline, in real terms, of nearly 40 per cent.

National (routine) spending

An examination of Conservative Central Office accounts, which are available from 1950 onwards, shows that spending has, in broad terms, remained constant. In 1984–7 Central Office expenditure was at the same level in real terms as in 1952–5. Labour's national spending increased in real terms and by the eighties approached that of Conservative Central Office (see Table 7.2).

Constituency (campaign) spending

Between 1949 and 1969, the legal ceiling on permitted expenditure by parliamentary candidates remained unchanged. Since they were years of rapid inflation, this limit therefore became much more stringent in real terms. Largely because of this, the cost of parliamentary election campaigns fell sharply. In 1987, Conservative candidates spent an average of £4,000 compared with £12,200 in 1945 (at June 1987 values). Similarly, average spending by Labour candidates declined, in real terms, from £9,300 to £3,900 and spending by Liberals (Alliance) dropped from £8,300 to £3,400. The cost of electioneering was also reduced by the fact that the election deposit remained at £150 until the 1987 general election, by which time its value had been greatly eroded by inflation. Since the 1987 election the deposit has risen to £500 but fewer candidates have had to forfeit it since the percentage of votes required to avoid forfeiture has dropped from 12.5 to 5 per cent.

In 1945, Conservative candidates were still frequently required by constituency associations to meet the bulk of their election expenses. The falling cost of local campaigning, combined with the fact that the Conservative candidates have been barred by party rules introduced before the 1950 general election from contributing to their own campaigns have greatly reduced the financial burdens on those wishing to enter Parliament.

In 1948, the Conservatives set up a Special Committee on Party Organisation under Sir David Maxwell-Fyfe (later Lord Kilmuir). The Committee's Report, adopted in 1949, limited a parliamentary candidate's annual subscription to his or her constituency association to £25 a year and stipulated that 'no subscription shall be made directly or indirectly by the candidate to the fund for statutory election expenses'. The reform was intended to open the way for working-class Conservatives to stand as parliamentary candidates. However, though the financial barriers have been removed, few working men have stood as Conservative candidates for the House of Commons.

An important effect of the falling costs of constituency electioneering has been to make it easier for the Liberal and Social Democrats to field a full list of candidates. For Labour, the drop in the burden of backing candidates has made it possible for trade unions to direct a growing percentage of their political levies to the national Labour Party organisation.

National (campaign) spending

The costs of national election campaigns have fluctuated wildly. The campaigns of 1945, 1950, 1951 and 1955 were inexpensive by the standards of some prewar elections. The development of advertising by Conservative Central Office in 1957–9 and in 1963–4 escalated costs. Yet, contrary to the predictions of the time, the 1959 and 1964 elections did not usher in an era of ever-increasing central campaign expenditures. It was not until 1987 that central election spending again approached, in real terms, the levels of 1964.

One reason why central campaign costs have not surged (in contrast to the experience of some other countries) has been the spread in the fifties of television ownership. Since television has become the most potent medium of political communication and since political parties are banned by law from purchasing advertising time on television, its growth has arguably limited the scope for high campaign spending.

What is the impact of party funding?

The way in which parties raise and spend money may potentially affect political life in a number of ways. Unfortunately political scientists have not found any agreed way to assess its actual impacts and there is much disagreement and confusion about the topic. The problem arises partly because it is difficult to separate the influence of money from other factors.

Party finance may be important in these ways:

1. Money spent on election campaigns may enable parties and candidates to win more votes.
2. Contributions may affect policy-making by making parties alter their policies and administrative decisions to fit the interest or demands of donors.
3. Control over money may affect the internal structure of power within a political party.
4. The cost of campaigning may influence political recruitment. If it is expensive to stand for Parliament, men and women without personal resources may be prevented from putting themselves forward.

This chapter will briefly consider the first of these categories only – the possible influence of campaign spending on voting. At constituency level, the influence of money is limited by the low ceilings on permitted expenditure by candidates at parliamentary elections. As mentioned earlier, expenditures by candidates of the different parties are broadly similar. In marginal constituencies, where spending is most likely to tip the balance, all the main parties tend to spend more than average and to approach the legal limit. Moreover, according to a common argument, the results of local campaigns depend more on the voluntary efforts of party workers than on expenditure on printing the election address or on other items of advertising.

Statistical analyses by R. J. Johnston suggest, however, that parliamentary candidates gain votes by spending more than their opponents. Had all Conservative, Labour and Alliance candidates spent to the legal limit in the 1983 general election, the outcome of no less than thirty constituency contests would probably have been altered, he argues. In particular, Alliance candidates would have benefited by spending as much as their opponents. Johnston is himself cautious about these conclusions and other scholars have disputed the applicability of statistical analyses such as those which he uses.

There is no statistical method of assessing the impact of spending on national campaigning. The importance of money in the national campaign is arguably limited for several reasons. Firstly, there has not been a consistent escalation in the costs (in real terms) of national campaigns. Even though the central Conservative and Labour campaigns of 1987 were more costly than central campaigns in other recent elections, the cost of the Labour campaign was not significantly higher than in 1964, while the Conservative campaign was lower in cost than in 1964 and 1935. Secondly, the fact that parties receive allocations of free television time limits the impact of paid newspaper advertising. Thirdly, the most important influences on election outcomes are arguably the news reports on television and radio and in the Press. The national party organisations do not pay for these either. The exposure gained by the Liberals and Social Democrats in most recent elections through media for which they have not had to pay helps to explain why they have increased their popularity during most recent election campaigns.

Should the system of party finance be reformed?

The issue of legal reform of the regulations relating to party finance was raised by the Labour government which came to power in 1974. It set up a Committee on Financial Aid to Political Parties under the chairmanship of a former cabinet minister, Lord Houghton. In 1976, the Houghton Committee proposed a system of public subsidies for parties, but the Labour government failed to devise an agreed scheme for state aid before it left office in 1979. Subsequently, the issues of reform were considered by two influential independent committees associated with the Hansard Society for Parliamentary Government and the Constitutional Reform Centre (*Paying for Politics*, 1981 and *Company Donations to Political Parties: A Suggested Code of Practice*, 1985).

Proposed reforms have included:

1. State financial subsidies to party organisations and candidates in the form of block grants.

2. Public subsidies given as grants matching small individual donations to parties.
3. Ceilings on permitted election spending by national party organisations.
4. Compulsory publication of national party accounts.
5. A loan on political payments by unions and companies.
6. Regulation of political donations by companies along the lines of the rules governing payments by trade unions.

Labour sympathisers have generally proposed state aid as a supplement to existing institutional payments whereas Liberals and Social Democrats have favoured state aid as a substitute for union and company contributions.

The main arguments in favour of state aid are the following:

1. It would reduce the unfair financial edge enjoyed by the Conservatives.
2. It would reduce Conservative and Labour dependence upon their institutional backers.
3. It would make it possible for national party organisations to employ larger staffs, thereby improving the quality of policy-making.
4. It would enable the party organisations to concentrate upon the recruitment of new members and on political education rather than upon the time-wasting tasks of fundraising.
5. State subventions to parties and elections have successfully been introduced in about two dozen foreign countries.

Arguments against public subsidies are as follows:

1. The existing system is not grossly unfair. The Conservative lead over Labour is small and declining. The Conservative fundraising lead does not derive from corporate contributions but from the fact that Conservative membership is so much greater than that of the other parties. It is therefore fair and legitimate. Moreover, the existing system of free broadcasting time has the effect of equalising the advertising resources of the rival party organisations.
2. Dependence upon public subsidies would make parties bureaucratic and unresponsive to their members. They would also deter the collection of small contributions by the party organisations.

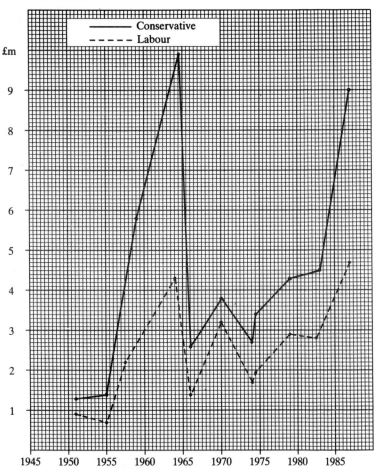

Figure 7.1 Conservative and Labour central expenditure on general election campaigns, 1951–87 (at constant June 1987 prices)

3. There is no evidence that the quality of policymaking by political parties is related to the size of their research staffs.

4. State finance would not reduce the dependence of the main parties on unions and companies unless the introduction of public subsidies were to be linked with a ban on institutional political contributions. Labour party supporters would be unwilling to endorse such a move.

5. Each party would attempt to pass laws in accordance with its

own interests. An undesirable process of 'legal gerrymandering' would ensue.

Whatever the merits of such opposing arguments, it is clear that there will be no move to introduce state aid to political parties while a Conservative government remains in power but that the issue would be raised if other parties were to enter office.

Bibliography

Bogdanor, V. (1982) 'Reflections on British political finance', *Parliamentary Affairs*, Vol. 35.

Bogdanor, V. (1984) 'Financing political parties in Britain', in V. Bogdanor (ed.) *Parties and Democracy in Britain and America*, Praeger.

Committee on Financial Aid to Political Parties (1976) *Report*, Cmnd 6601, HMSO (Houghton Report).

Constitutional Reform Centre and the Hansard Society for Parliamentary Government (1985) *Company Donations to Political Parties: A Suggested Code of Practice*, CRC.

Ewing, K. (1987) *The Funding of Political Parties in Britain*, Cambridge University Press.

Gordon, I. and Whiteley, P. (1980) 'Comment: Johnston on campaign expenditure and the efficacy of advertising', *Political Studies*, Vol. 28.

Hansard Society for Parliamentary Government (1981) *Paying for Politics: The Report of the Commission upon the Financing of Political Parties*.

Johnston, R. J. (1986) 'A further look at British political finance', *Political Studies*, Vol. 34.

Johnston, R. J. (1987) *Money and Votes: Constituency Campaign Spending and Election Results*, Croom Helm.

Pinto-Duschinsky, M. (1981) *British Political Finance 1930–1980*, American Enterprise Institute.

Pinto-Duschinsky, M. (1985) 'Trends in British political funding, 1979–1983', *Parliamentary Affairs*, Vol. 38.

Pinto-Duschinsky, M. (1989) 'Trends in British party funding, 1983–1987', *Parliamentary Affairs*, Vol. 42.

8

The Party System in Northern Ireland Since 1945

PAUL ARTHUR

'The end of the world would have occasioned only a little more alarm' was the response of one lady to what she saw as Labour's cataclysmic victory in the 1945 general election.[1] 1945 was not an *annus mirabili* in Northern Ireland. In two general elections (one for the local Parliament at Stormont, the other for Westminster) the hub of the universe remained 'the dreary steeples of Fermanagh and Tyrone', to quote Winston Churchill's wonderment at the longevity and integrity of the quarrel in Ulster.

Electoral predictability and an artificial stability

Electoral predictability had been and remained the name of the game in the province. In the June 1945 election for Stormont, no less than 20 of the 52 seats were uncontested, with the Unionist Party winning 33 and the Nationalists 10, followed by a melange of 'socialists' comprising Northern Ireland Labour, Commonwealth Labour, Independent Labour and Socialist Republican. A similar trend was evident in July with Unionists winning nine of the 13 Westminster seats. The only surprise concerned the two victorious Nationalist candidates. Both had been elected in 1935 but had not taken their seats. Now, with the misplaced confidence

that the new Labour government would be good for Irish nationalism, they recognised the efficacy of participation.

It was the same perception which mobilised the Unionist
community into conducting one of its perennial debates about the
status of Northern Ireland within the United Kingdom. With the
partition of Ireland in 1920 Unionists had been reluctant devolutionists, but became converts to strong regional government in the
intervening years. The strength of their sense of regional identity
serves as a useful barometer of their constitutional confidence.

Hence, with the return in 1945 of a government considered to
be suspect on the Union, the Northern Ireland Cabinet wondered,
in the words of Prime Minister Sir Basil Brooke, 'whether any
changes could be made to avert such a situation [a constitutional
clash between Belfast and London]. Two possibilities were domi-
nion status for Northern Ireland and a return to Westminster'. But
the Cabinet soon realised that the British government was staffed
by 'practical and experienced men who are personally friendly to
Ulster'. And Unionists recognised that they had secured the best
of all possible worlds by gaining autonomy of decision-making for
Northern Ireland within the constraints imposed by economic
dependence on the rest of the UK.[2]

We have lingered on the 1945 general election to make a
number of (seemingly paradoxical) points. Firstly, Labour's victory was not the watershed in Northern Ireland that it had been
in Britain. Admittedly it caused mild paroxysms for the Unionist
government, but these were dispelled once Labour showed a clean
pair of hands. It meant that Westminster was perceived again as
being marginal to Northern Ireland's interest and that the 'real'
political debate would unfold at Stormont. It was as if Northern
Ireland was hermetically sealed, the Albania of the western world.

Secondly, notwithstanding the number of socialist parties prepared to contest elections, class was not the primary source of
allegiance in Northern Ireland. The 'constitutional question' –
defined in terms of national identity and religious affiliation –
decided the outcome of elections. Hence, the Northern Ireland
Labour Party (NILP), prominent after 1958, was swept aside in
the late sixties when the demands of the civil rights movement
were perceived as being a (covert republican) challenge to the
regime.

Thirdly, electoral competition was concentrated largely on a struggle for power at Stormont where Unionists never held less than 32 of the 52 seats. The result was an artificial stability in the years 1921–69 when even the dogs in the street could have predicted the electoral outcome. But events since 1968 have demonstrated that Unionism's internal identity and sense of discipline were not quite as strong as many imagined. One of the factors which challenged Unionism's hegemony was the creeping realisation that there were *three* sites of power: besides Stormont there were also local councils and Westminster.

Local councils, the bulk of which were Unionist controlled, represented an alternative focus of allegiance in a party which was formed from the bottom up and in a confrontational society. They guarded their limited powers jealously, provided leadership of the grassroots, and exercised a restraining role on the party, especially when it betrayed 'progressive' (that is, compromising) tendencies. That sort of behaviour might be expected at Westminster but it had low visibility in the province and no one paid much attention to it until the seventies. But with the imposition of direct rule and the prorogation of Stormont in 1972, Westminster became the *only* site of power and those who sat there enjoyed privileged status.

Political behaviour and intra-ethnic conflict

It is a paradox of political life in Northern Ireland that the minority community – represented by different Irish Nationalist parties – has always displayed a greater degree of communal self-confidence than the majority which had enjoyed one-party dominance for more than 50 years. Part of the explanation lies in the narrow Unionist perspective of ignoring the political realities outside the province. So long as they could keep Stormont in existence nothing else mattered.

From the outset they adopted a defensive mentality – 'what we have, we hold'. Their politics has been built on reacting to unwelcome developments: against the Third Home Rule Bill from 1912 onwards; against the Republic of Ireland's claims to Northern Ireland's territory; against the Catholic minority within the province which they considered to be a fifth column; against the imposition of direct rule in 1972 and British 'interference' in the province's affairs; and against the gradualist Anglo-Irish scenario which followed the signing of the Hillsborough Agreement in November 1985.

With the advantage of hindsight we can say that Unionists felt confident only between 1921 and the outbreak of 'the troubles' in 1969. Even within that period – as we have seen with reaction to the 1945 general election – there were moments of genuine self-doubt. Indeed, we might follow the line of reasoning of the historian David Miller[3] that the political and historical experience of the Ulster Protestant community since the plantations of the seventeenth century has led them to proclaim (loudly) loyalty to the British Sovereign *on their own terms.* Their allegiance to the British political system was, and is, conditional. The same, of course, could be said of Nationalists. They have impressively long memories and a political behaviour which predates partition, but no one has been in any doubt that they ever proclaimed primary allegiance to the United Kingdom.

The innocent observer studying Northern Ireland politics from the outside would be forgiven for assuming that it followed the British model. After all, it was a product of mass democracy, it had free, open elections and there appeared to be a two-party system (with numerous minor parties following in its wake). However, there were differences. Besides the complication of studying elections at local, provincial, national and, latterly, European levels (all of which were contested with impressive intensity), the difficulty is compounded by a lack of uniformity in the types of electoral system.

The British plurality system is used only for Westminster elections. The single transferrable vote system (STV) of proportional representation is used at constituency level for local and provincial elections. STV is utilised for the direct elections to the European Parliament but in this case Northern Ireland is treated as one constituency. By most standards, therefore, the electoral system is a deviant case in the British model. Proportional representation has been introduced twice – from partition until the Unionist government abolished it before the 1929 Stormont general election, and after the imposition of direct rule in 1972. On both occasions British interest in the Northern Ireland problem was high, and that has always spelt trouble for the Unionist community.

There were other anomalies. Northern Ireland did not follow the British postwar practice of introducing universal suffrage at local government level until 1969, something which was used to abuse Unionist claims to be British. But this did not alter the facts that Unionists remained permanently in power and the opposition was plaintive, fragmented and futile. The largest, the Nationalist Party, lacked direction and organisation – an absence of paid officials, of central party headquarters and even (until November 1964) of an election manifesto. Its policy was based on a sense of manifest destiny that Irish unity was 'inevitable'.

On the other hand, permanent power brought an inevitable arrogance to the Unionists. They did not need negotiating skills; they did not engage in dialogue with their own supporters about the unfinished business of partition and its aftermath; nor did they recognise danger signals such as the build-up of the civil rights' campaign in the late sixties. Instead they relied on the divided opposition, the benign neglect of successive British governments and an electoral system inimical to minority interests.

All of that began to change with the Civil Rights Movement. Harold Wilson responded by persuading the Northern Ireland Prime Minister to embark on a reform programme. Captain O'Neill's problem was that he could not bring a significant segment of his own party with him, and so reform was a painful business, creating deeper community polarisation, British exasperation and a fragmentation of the Unionist monolith. The result was the imposition of direct rule in 1972 as a temporary expedient.

An early decision of the new administration was the reintroduction of proportional representation. It had been a feature of the Government of Ireland Act (1920) as a device to give the minority a fairer deal, but was abolished by the Unionists for local government elections in 1922 and for Stormont in 1929. Its re-introduction was meant to encourage the growth of middle politics, but it unwittingly presented loyalists with a lifeline. The middle ground, occupied by the bi-confessional Alliance Party (founded in 1970), proved to be illusory. The Alliance has played a crucial role at critical junctures such as the formation of the power-sharing Executive in 1974 and in signalling *some* Protestant support for the Anglo-Irish Agreement, but it is perceived as being a comfortable middle-class party confined to the greater Belfast area.

Instead proportional representation has muddied the waters by creating a multi-party system and by emphasising the intensity of the intra-ethnic conflict. The split in the Unionist community since the O'Neill reform programme developed with the power-sharing Executive of 1974. It was opposed by 27 loyalists in a 78-seat Assembly, and when the failed Assembly was replaced by a Constitutional Convention, established 'to consider what provisions for the government of Northern Ireland would be likely to command the most widespread acceptance throughout the community', anti-power sharing loyalists won 47 seats under the umbrella of the United Ulster Unionist Council (UUUC). The UUUC, formed in January 1974 to oppose power sharing and Irish government interference in Northern Ireland affairs, collapsed in 1977 following a 'constitutional stoppage' led by the Rev. Ian Paisley and Protestant paramilitaries in an effort to persuade the authorities to restore Stormont and to take the offensive against the IRA.

The very existence of the UUUC represented an innovation in Unionist politics – the emergence of a coalition. In turn that signalled the disarray of the Protestant community: for the first time since 1921 no single party dominated that community. Ian Paisley's Democratic Unionist Party (DUP), founded in 1971, sought that domination – a position *he* believed *he* had attained after a massive personal victory in the first direct elections to the European Parliament in 1979, a result he interpreted as a 'twentieth-century miracle' engineered by the mysterious providence of God.

In fact, while this popularity cannot be gainsaid, the DUP's onward march into the establishment citadel has been reversed in more recent years by the Ulster Unionist Party's (UUP) adoption of militant policies. The DUP had offered certainty and conviction in a period of considerable doubt. What it lacked in consistency – policy veered between devolution, integration and independence – it compensated for in militancy in alliance with paramilitaries (tacit and otherwise) in 1974, 1977, 1981 and in the aftermath of the Hillsborough Agreement after 1985. Even when this approach failed abjectly, as in 1977, Paisley's appeal held because he was considered to be ideologically sound. All of that changed, however, with the signing of the Anglo-Irish Agreement.

Party competition and the Anglo-Irish Agreement

The 1985 Hillsborough Agreement has had two effects – one profound and one recurring – on Unionist electoral competition. Firstly, the old confrontational tactics appear to have failed. Massive street protests, local council boycotts, Westminster abstention, parliamentary violence and intimidation, unofficial referenda: all have failed to move Prime Minister Thatcher in her support of the Agreement. There is no precedent for such failure in Unionist mythology and leadership has had to face the fundamental question of the meaning of 'Unionism' which entails responsibilities and obligations as well as the advantages of being in the Union. The alternative is 'loyalism' with one's primary loyalty to the concept of 'Ulster'. In the past many in the Protestant community saw themselves as Unionist but behaved as loyalist.

Secondly, since Hillsborough a (highly personalised) loyalist coalition has re-emerged in an effort to prevent a serious Unionist split. We need to remember that since 1970 ten new parties have been established, six of which were Unionist, although at present competition is primarily between the UUP and the DUP. The UUP remains dominant but realises that it cannot afford to relax. It is in this context that the alliance forged between James Molyneaux and Ian Paisley becomes relevant. Both were fundamentally opposed to the Agreement: there the unanimity ends. Molyneaux's UUP is divided between devolutionists and integrationists; many of the rank and file were unhappy with the DUP's extra-parliamentary behaviour. On the other hand, the pact meant the absence of electoral competition with the DUP, the value of which became clear at the 1987 general election – two UUP seats were vulnerable to a DUP challenge but both were held because of the pact.

By spring 1989, a condition of stasis had come to exist in the Unionist community. The two leaders were locked in a paralysed embrace and secondary leadership was showing signs of disquiet. Two momentary shafts of wisdom lightened the darkness: the Ulster Political Research Group's (UPRG) *Common Sense* and a joint Unionist report entitled *An End To Drift*. The source of the *Common Sense* document was as startling as its content: the UPRG was the 'think tank' of the paramilitary UDA which now seemed to be prepared to contemplate power sharing, and at last symbolised that loyalists must resort to brain power rather than brawn if they were to find a place in the sun.

Common Sense was published in January 1987 and served as a precursor for the joint Unionist report published in June. Written by the deputy leaders of the two parties and by the Chief Executive of the UUP, *An End To Drift* was not specific about solutions but was sufficiently flexible to imply that negotiation rather than confrontation was the way forward. Neither leader recognised the significance of the two documents but both were left with the dilemma – what can we do to persuade the Thatcher government to reconsider the Anglo-Irish Agreement?

Party competition inside the Catholic community can be summarised more briefly. Until the civil rights campaign, the Catholic community was noted for its passivity and lack of coherence. It made little electoral impact and, with the exception of the 1921 provincial elections, did not even put up enough candidates to form an alternative government. Sinn Fein had a policy of 'principled abstention' and the Nationalist Party one of intermittent abstention. The foundation of the Social Democratic and Labour Party (SDLP) in August 1970 presented constitutional Nationalists with the opportunity to contribute to Northern Ireland politics for the first time since partition.

SDLP success – it is the only Nationalist party to have been in government in the province, and it is in a position where it cannot be ignored by government – can be explained by its professionalism and by the initial lack of an alternative. Professionalism is an under-utilised commodity in provincial politics. Unionism needed little more than an electoral machine, and Nationalism did not even have that. The nature of the SDLP is part modernising with a formal commitment to bring about 'the public ownership and democratic control of such essential services as the common good requires' and membership of the Socialist International. But it is also part traditional, aiming 'to promote the cause of Irish unity based on the consent of the majority of people in Northern Ireland'. The dual identity contributes to its tenacity.

With the collapse of the 1974 power-sharing Executive, following the Ulster Workers' Council strike and Unionist unwillingness to contemplate power sharing, the SDLP sustained itself by emphasising the Irish and (latterly) the international dimensions of the problem. These became of vital importance in the eighties when the party's monopoly of Nationalist politics was challenged. The Irish Independence Party, formed in 1977, offered some competition on a more militant platform but it never won more than 4 per cent of the vote and it was soon overtaken by Sinn Fein.

Provisional Sinn Fein (PSF) eschewed the electoral process largely until the hunger strikes in 1980 and 1981. The hunger strikes brought out tens of thousands in protest. PSF, which had been undergoing a fundamental review of strategy in any case, calculated that Republicanism could win the battle of persuading the British to withdraw but would be likely to lose the political initiative to the constitutional Nationalist parties which would take power in the new Ireland. Party strategists decided that PSF should be more than a support group to the IRA and that it should become a fully-fledged political movement capable of taking power at the requisite moment. Once it contested elections, its rise from an electoral base of zero was spectacular. Soon it was the fourth largest party in the local councils and was taking as much as 40 per cent of the Catholic vote. Gerry Adams was returned as MP for Belfast West in 1983 to match the single SDLP representative at Westminster. In the following general election in 1987 the SDLP increased its Westminster representation to three and cut into Adams' majority in Belfast West. This (temporary?) reverse in fortunes can be explained by a consideration of external factors, a matter of some importance in any attempt to understand the party system in Northern Ireland.

Nationalist politics had been fuelled by a perception of adversity and denial. As a permanent minority it could not expect justice. The Nationalist Party did little except to engage in a recurrent whine. The SDLP used the political process and when it had been denied its just deserts (as in 1974) it set out to change the parameters of the problem. It invoked the assistance of the Republic's constitutional Nationalist parties through the New Ireland Forum, a body engaged in a rigorous analysis of late twentieth-century Irish nationalism, which met in 1983–4. The Forum gave the SDLP a role and a visibility at a time when it was redundant in Northern Ireland, and gave constitutional National-ism a respectability in the international arena. As a result, the flagging Anglo-Irish process was given a boost culminating in the signing of the Agreement at Hillsborough Castle in November 1985. The SDLP had turned adversity on its head, and the

Agreement had changed the rules of the political game in Northern Ireland.

The post-Hillsborough losers were armed Republicanism and the Unionist family. Republicans had exploited adversity in the past by explaining their failure to achieve power as the result of British manipulation and repression. It responded by imposing its own repression through the armed struggle and, more recently, the strategy of the 'Armalite and the ballot box'. But that strategy contained its own inherent contradictions and has led to a split, with the creation of Republican Sinn Fein in 1987. At present, the Republican movement is engaged in an internal discussion about its future.

The depth of Unionist reaction to the Agreement illustrates its sense of hurt and betrayal. We have noted the nature of that reaction through the two documents. Another manifestation has been the formation of a pressure group, the Campaign for Equal Citizenship (CEC), intent, it maintains, on breaking down sectarian politics in the province by persuading the British *national* parties to organise and contest seats in Northern Ireland, as in any other part of the UK. It has had little success and there is no evidence that the national parties want to organise in the province. They note that Unionists were happy with their (devolved) lot between 1921 and 1972, when Stormont demonstrated that Northern Ireland was *not* like the rest of the UK. In addition Unionist leaders have been used to a simulacrum of power. They are reluctant to relinquish that and they are not certain how far they can trust their constitutional fate to British politicians in an integrated system.

Conclusion: an aberrant case in UK politics

The thrust of this chapter is that Northern Ireland is *sui generis*. Political allegiances are not along the familiar right–left spectrum. Its subordinate status within the United Kingdom was not apparent to its political leaders during most of the period 1921–69 so that they behaved as if they were ruling a sovereign state. The shock of direct rule with the prorogation of Stormont in 1972 and, latterly, the impact of the Anglo-Irish Agreement has induced a crisis of identity within the majority community and encouraged many in the minority that Irish unity is a feasible objective. Its ambivalence towards political violence, its peculiar political development and its present state of political limbo all help to explain the eccentricities of the party system in Northern Ireland.

Comparison with Scotland and Wales is superfluous. Even when the Nationalist parties were doing well in the periphery of Britain no one really imagined that their success would lead to the breakup of the United Kingdom and no one expected them to operate other than within the law. Moreover, it was evident that the government wished them to remain within the British political system. The same certainty cannot be found in Northern Ireland. Even those who call themselves Unionists doubt whether there is a *British* commitment to the Union. For their part, successive governments at Westminster have known that a substantial segment of the minority desire Irish unity whereas many in the majority community consider the present price of the Union – an insistence that the Westminster model must be abandoned in favour of power sharing – is too much to pay.

For too long Northern Ireland has been outside the mainstream of British political practice. It was an arrangement which was considered mutually advantageous. This policy of benign neglect reinforced the impression that Northern Ireland was indeed a place apart. While the fundamental constitutional question remains to be settled, the Northern Ireland party system will be an aberrant case in United Kingdom politics.

Notes

1. Cited in Marwick, A. (1982) *British Society Since 1945*, p. 102, Allen Lane.
2. This paragraph relies on Harkness, D. (1983) *Northern Ireland Since 1920*, pp. 106–8, Helicon.
3. This concept is discussed at length in Miller, D. W. (1978) *Queen's Rebels. Ulster Loyalism in Historical Perspective*, Gill and Macmillan.

Key Dates since 1968

1968 Civil Rights Campaign, with the demand for 'one man one vote' at local government elections.
1969 Universal suffrage granted at local council level.

1970   Alliance Party formed in April; the Social Democrats and Labour Party (SDLP) founded in August.

1971   Democratic Unionist Party founded in September.

1972   Stormont prorogued and direct rule imposed in March.

1973   Proportional representation introduced for the first time since 1929 for elections to 26 new district councils in May; and for the 78-seat Northern Assembly in June.

1974   Power-sharing Executive for Northern Ireland Assembly meets on 1 January and collapses before the end of May as a result of the UWC strike.

1980   Two Anglo-Irish summits in May and December to establish closer relations between the two countries. Republicans in the Maze Prison begin their first hunger strike, which is called off in December.

1981   Second hunger strike begins with the death of ten protestors before it is called off in September.

1982   Elections in October for a Northern Ireland Assembly. PSF wins five seats and 10 per cent of the vote. The SDLP wins fourteen seats. Both parties boycott the Assembly.

1983   Provisional Sinn Fein wins its first Westminster seat in Belfast at the June general election.

1985   The Anglo-Irish Agreement is signed at Hillsborough Castle on 15 November.

1987   Westminster general election in May. Adams holds West Belfast for PSF and SDLP increases its representation from one to three, both gains at the expense of the UUP.

9

Scottish and Welsh Nationalist Parties Since 1945

JAMES G. KELLAS

Party politics in Scotland and Wales differ from English party politics. Both Scotland and Wales are nations with separate political institutions and a strong sense of national consciousness.

Nationalist parties and British parties

Not only has this produced Nationalist parties – the Scottish National Party (SNP) and Plaid Cymru (PC) – but it has also led to the British parties adopting national forms in Scotland and Wales. After 1945 the Liberal Party adopted a structure in which the Scottish and Welsh parties had virtual independence, although closely linked through the parliamentary party. The successor party, the Social and Liberal Democrats, is a federal party, with the Scottish and Welsh Democrats having autonomy in Scottish and Welsh matters.

The Labour Party and the Conservative Party also have Scottish and Welsh organisations and hold conferences in Scotland and Wales, although these are not as independent as those of the Liberals/SLD. Even so, the Labour and Conservative Parties are often at pains to emphasise the special character of their operations in the non-English nations, although their party organisations are ultimately controlled from London. The terms 'Scottish Labour Party' and 'Scottish Conservative Party' are used in electioneering, the latter being the official term in Conservative Party political broadcasts for Scotland alone (the Labour Party uses 'The Labour Party in Scotland' in that context).

The explanation for this distinct party activity in Scotland and Wales lies not only in the separateness of Scotland and Wales in the system of government, but also in the special political culture and electoral behaviour in these nations. The separate governmental structure, seen most clearly in the existence of the Scottish and Welsh Offices in Edinburgh and Cardiff respectively, and underpinned by separate systems of local government, education, and the National Health Service, as well as a separate legal system and Established Church in the case of Scotland, leads to special Scottish and Welsh political issues developing which have to be dealt with by all the parties. They must discuss these issues at their conferences in Scotland and Wales, and produce party programmes and manifestos outlining their Scottish and Welsh policies.

All the parties other than the Nationalist parties are, of course, 'British' parties, and they operate at the British level as well. The balance of power between the British and Scottish/Welsh organisations in the parties is tilted overwhelmingly to the British end. The leaders of the British parties control the party organisations and have the decisive voice in drawing up the party manifestos. Nevertheless, there is a territorial tension within the British parties, and an attempt is made to produce a consensus among the nations, rather than to seem to force the Scottish and Welsh party organisations into conformity with the British leadership.

For example, the adoption of the policy of devolution to Scotland in the Labour Party in 1974 depended on a show of endorsement from the Scottish party conference, and the community charge ('poll tax') was adopted by the Conservative government after a revolt at the Scottish Conservative conference in 1985 concerning the impact of rating revaluation.

Objectives of SNP and Plaid Cymru

Only the Nationalists can claim, therefore, to be strictly 'Scottish and Welsh parties' as their electioneering is confined to their respective nations. They have members and sympathisers in England, but so far, they have not put up any candidates in England, and their view of the British Parliament is that it is in reality an 'English' Parliament. They do, however, seek representation there, and to that extent are supportive of constitutional conventions framed for the British Constitution. This co-option into the British system is seen by them as *pro tempore* until a majority of the people of Scotland/Wales decide otherwise. The SNP interprets this as meaning when the SNP wins a majority of Scottish seats at Westminster, but in 1987 it added the provision that such a majority would lead it to 'cooperate with other Scottish MPs over the transfer of power to the Scottish Parliament and arrange a written constitution to be prepared' which 'will be put to the Scottish people by means of a Referendum' (1987 General Election Manifesto, *Play the Scottish Card*, p. 7).

Plaid Cymru, in its 1987 manifesto, has more limited aims. In that election it campaigned for a Welsh Senate 'to assume all the powers of the Secretary of State within the Welsh Office' (1987 General Election Programme, *Winning for Wales*, p. 24). However, its long-term aim is 'full self-government for Wales by establishing a democratic socialist state'. It would achieve Wales' right to govern itself 'by winning the support of a majority of her people' (*Plaid Cymru Aims, c.* 1983). However, in the Plaid Cymru–Scottish National Party Agreement of 1987, it was stated that 'in the event of either Party obtaining a majority of seats in their respective countries, the other Party shall support that Party in fulfilling its constitutional mandate – independence for Scotland and self-government for Wales' (section 1). As we shall see, these aims and tactics have varied at different general elections. The participation of the SNP and PC in the House of Commons is in marked contrast to the abstentionism of Provisional Sinn Fein, the political wing of the IRA.

There are some extreme Nationalists in Scotland and Wales, but they have remained a minor force in electoral politics.[1]

The principal feature of Scottish and Welsh nationalism, however, from the point of view of party politics, is the dominance over nationalist politics which the SNP and PC have achieved within their respective countries. There are no other nationalist parties of any significance. Very few nationalist movements in the world have managed to keep within the bounds of one political party all the different kinds of nationalism, left and right, and moderate and fundamentalist. This has not been achieved without a history of tensions and temporary schisms, however. Yet the main picture is one of unity behind one nationalist party.

Distinctive characters of Welsh and Scottish nationalism

While there are many similarities between the Scottish and Welsh Nationalist Parties, which have led them at times into close collaboration in election campaigns and in the House of Commons, there are also striking differences. These differences come largely from the contrasting characters of the Scottish and Welsh nations, and their relationship to England.

Scotland is today a nation of 5 million people, and the 1981 census shows that 90 per cent were born there. Wales has 2.8 million people, but only 80 per cent were born there. As Scottish and Welsh nationalism are directed towards removing 'English control' it is significant to note that while 6 per cent of the Scottish population in 1981 was English-born, as many as 17 per cent of the Welsh population were in that category. There has been considerable migration to Wales in the eighties, much of it to the predominantly Welsh-speaking areas, so that in 1989 the figure of 17 per cent is under-stated. This has been seen by Welsh nationalists and others as a threat to the majority status of the Welsh language in these areas.

Although there is greater national homogeneity in the population of Scotland than there is in Wales, and less disturbance through migration from England, there has been in recent years talk of 'the Englishing of Scotland', whereby top jobs in Scottish institutions are seen to go to English people, and decisions are made which ignore Scottish distinctiveness. Appeals to nationalism in Scotland have the potential support of nine-tenths of the people (assuming that all Scottish-born people share national identity), but in Wales such appeals are likely to be more divisive, especially if they seek to exclude English people, or non-Welsh speakers, from membership of the Welsh nation.

This highlights the fact that Welsh nationalism is closely bound up with the Welsh language. Although only 18.9 per cent of the Welsh population could speak Welsh in 1981 (cf. 1951, 28.9 per cent; 1961, 26 per cent; 1971, 20.8 per cent), there are areas of Wales where Welsh speaking is widespread. These are concentrated in the northwest (e.g. Gwynedd, 61.2 per cent; Dyfed, 46.3 per cent: 1981 figures). It is no accident that this was the area which returned three Welsh Nationalist MPs in 1987 (Caernarfon; Meirionnydd Nant Conwy; Ynys Môn). The other side of the coin is that the non-Welsh speaking areas are generally suspicious of Welsh nationalism, or perhaps more precisely Plaid Cymru, which they identify as seeking to impose the Welsh language on the non-Welsh speaking population. They are afraid that an independent Wales (or even a Wales with a devolved government) would be run largely by Welsh-speakers, with non-Welsh speakers discriminated against. It is this fear which largely explains the overwhelming 'No' vote (80 per cent) for a Welsh Assembly in 1979. This does not mean that the non-Welsh-speaking Welsh have no sense of national identity or nationalism. Rather, they avoid giving support to Plaid Cymru and express their Welsh nationalism through voting for Labour or the Liberals/Democrats. Thus, if the Welsh language gives Welsh nationalism its cultural strength, it also divides the Welsh nation politically.

Although it is not a political party, the Welsh Language Society (Cymdeithas Yr Iaith Gymraeg) rivals Plaid Cymru as the voice of Welsh nationalism. Formed by a group of Plaid members in 1962, it has been the most important manifestation of linguistic nationalism in Wales and has engaged in civil disobedience campaigns including the bombing and burning of property, especially 'second homes' owned by English people, and transmitters of broadcasts in English. While this has at times proved to be an embarrassment to Plaid Cymru, which sticks to constitutional action, it has been a powerful reminder to the Plaid that there can be no back-sliding on the language question. As long as the Plaid believes that Welsh is the only national language of Wales, it must accept the Welsh Language Society's aims (if not its methods). That it may be changing its view on this vital matter will be seen later.

In contrast, there is no divisive language question in Scotland. English is spoken by 98.5 per cent of the Scottish population, though in the Western Isles and some northwestern mainland districts a majority speak Gaelic, a Celtic language related to Irish and Welsh. The SNP does not have the promotion of Gaelic as its central concern, although it does favour recognition of Gaelic as an official language in Scotland. The SNP therefore does not divide the Scottish nation along linguistic or even ethnic lines, but along lines which are primarily political and economic. On the whole, the SNP does not seek a 'Scotland for the Scots' led by a core of 'Scottish Scots', whose language is distinct from the English of the English. Rather it seeks a Scotland with political and economic independence, whose cultural identity, while distinct from that of England, is not tied to a separate national language. Welsh nationalism, on the other hand, is less strong on political and economic independence, while being insistent on Wales' linguistic and cultural identity.

All this reflects the different histories of Wales and Scotland. Wales lost its statehood through Union with England in 1536, and it did not retain many administrative, legal, educational and ecclesiastical institutions. Scotland, after the Union of 1707, kept such institutions, and its Union was 'quasi-federal' in theory, if not in practice. This has led to widely differing forms of national consciousness and nationalism in the two nations, even though both have as their aim the dissolution of the Union with England. Most importantly, the Scottish institutions have usually satisfied aspirations of Scottish nationalism within the British state, and their members have a vested interest in the status quo, as long as their position is not attacked by an English takeover. Welsh interests, on the other hand, are relatively new, and more nationalist. They are trying to break away from the British connection to form new vested interests. It is not yet clear to them whether the British state will protect them, as in the Scottish case, or seek to crush them. So far, these Welsh interests have proved weaker than their Scottish counterparts, although the Welsh language campaigners have scored some notable successes: place names in Wales have changed from English to Welsh in some areas, or are given in two languages; education in Welsh has been firmly established in many areas; and there has been a Welsh-language TV Channel since 1982, largely as a result of a threatened hunger strike by the PC President, Gwynfor Evans.

Electoral fortunes of SNP and Plaid Cymru since 1945

When we focus on the history of the SNP and PC since 1945, we see in each a parallel development of electoral success and party transformation.[2] Until the sixties, both parties were on the fringe of electoral politics, and took second place in nationalism to extra-parliamentary action, through petitions such as the Scottish Covenant (1949) and the Parliament for Wales Campaign (1954–56). The transformation to successful electoral activity began in 1959 for PC and 1961 for the SNP. New activists came on the scene, who transformed the party organisation, and inaugurated modern electioneering techniques – motorcades, party logos, mass canvasses. The Nationalist parties mobilised many young people, who were looking for a new politics to match the new social liberation of the sixties.

As a party wins votes and seats, so its nature changes. It becomes more credible, and it spawns a mass membership and a parliamentary party, whose relationship with the party organisation may be problematic. The party leaders may be out of tune with the members, and the MPs may feel that what is required at Westminster may be different from what the party back home has in mind. This was particularly so in 1979, when the SNP MPs were divided on their tactics over the Scotland Act after the referendum vote. Should they vote the Callaghan Government down, or sustain it while it prevaricated on what to do about the Scottish Assembly? In the event, they voted Labour out of office, a move which inspired Callaghan to say bitterly that the SNP were 'turkeys voting for an early Christmas'! This action of the SNP MPs was a clear example of the power of the parliamentary leader, Donald Stewart, to determine SNP strategy in the House of Commons, whatever opinion might be back in Scotland. It proved to be the end, not only for the Callaghan Government, but for devolution after the Thatcher Government was elected.

Electoral fortunes also affect the power structure within the party organisation. A party which is winning votes and seats does not normally turn on its leaders, and may invest them with great power. A party which is losing at the polls turns inward and seeks remedies, often by changing its leaders or its policies. Both the SNP and PC have moved from decentralisation to centralisation in party structure – more power has gone from the grassroots to the leaders; strategies have moved from fundamentalism to pragmatism; from centre to left (PC) and from left to centre (SNP). All these things have to be related to how the parties were faring in elections, and the power of the leadership to shape the parties to achieve electoral success.

Table 9.1 The performance of the Nationalist parties at general elections, 1945–87

(a) The SNP vote

Election	Candidates	MPs elected	% of Scottish vote
1945	8	0	1.2
1950	3	0	0.4
1951	2	0	0.3
1955	2	0	0.5
1959	5	0	0.8
1964	15	0	2.4
1966	23	0	5.0
1970	65	1	11.4
1974 (Feb.)	70	7	21.9
1974 (Oct.)	71	11	30.4
1979	71	2	17.3
1983	71	2	11.8
1987	71	3	14.0

Note: During this period, the SNP won by-elections in Motherwell (April 1945); Hamilton (November 1967); Govan (November 1973 and again in November 1988).

(b) The Plaid Cymru vote

Election	Candidates	MPs elected	% of Welsh vote
1945	7	0	1.2
1950	7	0	1.2
1951	4	0	0.7
1955	11	0	3.1
1959	20	0	5.2
1964	23	0	4.8
1966	20	0	4.3
1970	36	0	11.5
1974 (Feb.)	36	2	10.7
1974 (Oct.)	36	3	10.8
1979	36	2	8.1
1983	38	2	7.8
1987	38	3	7.3

Note: During this period, PC won a by-election at Carmarthen (July 1966).

The electoral fortunes of the SNP and PC from 1945 to 1987 show broadly similar trends at first sight. Both parties had negligible support at the polls until the sixties, peaked during the seventies, and fell back in the eighties. This might indicate common sources of nationalism in Scotland and Wales, and there is no doubt that such sources can be found. But there are also significant differences between the voting record for the SNP and the Plaid, as can be seen from Table 9.1.[3] The Plaid took off earlier than the SNP, in 1959 (5.2 per cent), and peaked in 197; (11.5 per cent). The SNP was nowhere nationally until 1966 (5.0 per cent), and peaked in October 1974 (30.4 per cent). The SNP retained its vote at a relatively high level in 1979 (17.3 per cent), compared with PC (8.1 per cent), and through to 1987 (SNP: 14.0 per cent, rising from 11.4 per cent in 1983; PC: 7.3 per cent, falling from 7.8 per cent in 1983).

Electoral geography in Wales and Scotland

Although both the SNP and PC claim to be 'national' parties, the pattern of their electoral support has always been uneven across the nations of Scotland and Wales. Both parties have done best in rural or small-town areas, and badly in cities and industrial areas except at by-elections. There is a difference between the SNP and PC in that the former has generally won a larger share of the vote, and has won some urban seats. It took Motherwell briefly at a by-election in 1945; the industrial seat of Hamilton at a by-election in 1967 (losing it in 1970); Glasgow Govan at a by-election in 1973 (losing it in February 1974 and winning it again at a by-election in November 1988); and Dundee East from February 1974 to 1987.[4] Plaid Cymru's seats, on the other hand, have all been in rural areas, mostly strong Welsh-speaking (Caernarvon/Caernarfon, February 1974–; Carmarthen, 1966–70, October 1974–9; Merioneth-shire/Meirionnydd Nant Conwy, February 1974–; Ynys Môn/ Anglesey, 1987–). There have been some good PC performances at by-elections in the industrial south of Wales (Rhondda West, 1967; Caerphilly, 1968; Merthyr Tydfil, 1972), but these were not sustained in the subsequent general elections. Similarly, the SNP's by-election victories at Hamilton (1967) and Govan (1973) were overturned by Labour gains at the following general elections.

This electoral record seems to point to a duality in nationalist electoral support. There is solid and permanent support in certain parts of the country, mostly rural, where nationalism represents an anti-Conservative vote which at times has gone to the Liberals. When the Liberals are strong, the nationalists tend to be weak.

Nationalist support seems to have been the result of 'tactical voting', with voters switching from their normal party to the nationalists in order to defeat the incumbent. This has been seen particularly in northeast Scotland and in Dundee East. In other areas, mostly urban, the nationalist parties have been able to draw on a 'protest vote', made up usually of discontented Labour supporters. They have not been able to retain all of this vote at general elections.

The appeal of SNP and Plaid Cymru

On the positive side, the nationalist parties have appealed to voters across all social classes who seek constitutional change for Scotland and Wales. In Scotland especially, there is a close correlation between SNP support and desire for a Scottish Parliament. Probably only a minority of SNP supporters wish for total independence for Scotland, according to the opinion polls. But very few support the constitutional status quo. The most widespread stated motive for voting SNP is that the party is 'good for Scotland'. This has not convinced anything near a majority of Scots to vote SNP, however, even in a good year for the party. The discovery and production of oil from the North Sea in the seventies gave the SNP the chance to appeal to the economic self-interest of the Scots. 'It's Scotland's Oil' and 'Rich Scots, Poor Britons' were SNP campaign slogans in 1974. Curiously enough, the SNP's oil campaign backfired. Most Scots remained convinced that the oil belonged to Britain as a whole, not just Scotland alone. But the oil issue did give people who supported devolution or independence before oil was discovered an added confidence, and may have contributed to the rise in SNP voting in the period 1974 to 1978.[5] At the same time, many were worried about the hostility of business to devolution and independence, and about the threat of companies pulling out of Scotland, were there to be home rule. When Labour put its devolution bills to the test of a referendum in 1979, many voters declined to vote Yes, and the nationalist parties lost votes in the 1979 election, especially the SNP.

Welsh nationalism has not been so concerned with economic questions, and there has been no oil issue. That is probably why the PC vote did not rise during the seventies in the manner of the

SNP vote. The Plaid has gained votes in areas threatened with industrial closures, and its manifestos have stressed economic development. But its decision to adopt a policy of 'a democratic state based on socialist principles' (1981) indicates an ideological affinity with Labour, even if its socialism is described as community-based, not the 'state centralism' of the Labour Party. This can be seen as an electoral weakness. While the Plaid can capture protest Labour voters when Labour appears to be powerless or abandoning socialist aims, it is not clearly an alternative to Labour, which acts almost like a Welsh nationalist party in its defence of the Welsh economy. For those Welsh nationalists who are not socialists, and who stress cultural or linguistic nationalism, PC socialist aims may be offensive, and may lead them to support the Democrats or avoid party politics altogether. They may feel more at home in the Welsh Language Society.

Organisation and membership

Unlike the major British parties, the nationalist parties are formally decentralised. Their constitutions vest authority in the members, not the leaders, and the basic unit of party organisation is the branch. There are around five hundred branches in the SNP and three hundred in the Plaid, and through representation at the national party conference they wield supreme power.[6] It is the party conference which decides on policy, elects the leaders, and controls the structure of the party. The SNP was successful in recruiting a mass membership in the sixties and seventies (its claimed membership of 120,000 in 1968 put it ahead of the other parties) although by the eighties this had largely disappeared. Plaid Cymru, on the other hand, never became a mass party, although its branches proliferated.[7]

Despite the formally decentralised nature of the SNP and PC, there is evidence in both parties of the operation of Michels' 'iron law of oligarchy'.[8] The leadership has expertise which the membership does not possess, and has a job to do running the party and winning elections, while the members are amateurs in politics. It also commands deference from the members, especially when the party is successful electorally. On the other hand, some observers (e.g. Roger Levy) have claimed that the SNP's organisational structure produces weak leadership and is unsuited to the task of presenting a vote-winning policy to the electorate.[9] Time and time again, the leadership has had to struggle to maintain unity and impose its will on the party. While this is to some extent true of all parties, the Nationalists' organisational structure has apparently made it more difficult for the leaders to retain control.

Factionalism

This is true particularly of the SNP where factions have continuously challenged the leadership. After the 1979 election losses, a '79 Group' was formed to press for a more radical or socialist policy. It was gradualist rather than fundamentalist, supporting devolution as a step to independence, which the fundamentalists rejected. Although the SNP had campaigned for a 'Yes' vote for the Scotland Act in the 1979 referendum, this had split the party, and in 1979 the conference resolved to have no more dealings with assemblies. In 1981, the conference supported a campaign of civil disobedience, and subsequently six 79 Group activists, including Jim Sillars, a former MP and the founder of the independent 'Scottish Labour Party' (1975–9), were fined for attempting to break into the unused Assembly Building in Edinburgh.

All this was a challenge to the moderate chairman of the party, Gordon Wilson, MP for Dundee East, who sought to establish his authority over the party. At the 1982 conference he demanded the expulsion of all factions in the party, on threat of his resignation. The conference rallied to his support, showing the power of the leader to get his way, even against prominent party activists such as Sillars, Margo MacDonald (ex-MP for Govan), and Stephen Maxwell. Wilson's power had previously been seen when he masterminded the party's Oil Campaign in 1974, and reformed the party organisation in the early sixties.

However, his success in 1982 did not conclusively defeat the '79 Group'. Its members were readmitted to the party, and their strategies were accepted by 1987. The SNP appeared to return to the support of gradualism by backing an elected Scottish Convention (Wilson's idea) which would probably recommend devolution rather than independence; in 1988 it sponsored civil disobedience in its campaign of non-payment of the poll tax (community

charge); and it retained a left-wing social and economic programme. It also supported Scotland's membership of the European Community ('Independence in Europe'), a reversal of its
opposition to the EC in the seventies.

By January 1989 this unity was in tatters. Jim Sillars' victory in
the Govan by-election (November 1988), overturning a 19,000
Labour majority on a platform of 'Independence in Europe', gave
added confidence to the fundamentalists in the party, who now
saw their aims as practical politics again. Jim Sillars, a powerful
orator and media performer, overshadowed the former leaders,
and he was reluctant to deal with other parties on a compromise
short of independence. Opinion poll support in Scotland for the
SNP rose to 32 per cent at the start of 1989, and this seemed to
point to another wave of Scottish nationalism, this time perhaps
unstoppable. But by now the SNP was committed to sitting down
with the other parties (except the Conservatives, who refused to
take part) at a Scottish Constitutional Convention to be organised
by the Campaign for a Scottish Assembly. While this was in line
with Wilson's gradualism, when the first planning meeting took
place on 27 January 1989, the SNP delegates (Wilson, Sillars and
Margaret Ewing, the Parliamentary leader) pulled out. They had
been allocated only 8 per cent of the delegates in a non-elected
Convention dominated by Labour. In this, the chance of the
'Independence in Europe' policy being endorsed was minimal, and
in any case it was not clear what would happen when the Thatcher
Government said No to the Convention's conclusions, as it surely
would. The pull-out revealed once more a split in the SNP, as
gradualists in the party complained that the SNP would isolate
itself from the bulk of home rule support in Scotland, which saw
devolution as a necessary first step to independence.

Plaid Cymru also illustrates the tension between a grassroots-
dominated constitution and a strong leadership. Here too the
conflicts are between fundamentalists and gradualists, socialists
and non-socialists, supporters of civil disobedience and of constitu-
tionalism. Yet, as Denis Balsom concludes, 'the picture that
emerges is of a centralised party structure where real influence lies
in the hands of relatively few people'.[10] Thus successive party
presidents, Saunders Lewis (1925–45), Gwynfor Evans (1945–81),
Dafydd Wigley (1981–4) and Dafydd Elis Thomas (1984–), have
stamped their ideology on the party. The President since 1984,

Dafydd Elis Thomas, MP for Meirionnydd Nant Conwy, has succeeded in moving the party in the direction he has wanted, despite opposition. He has moderated the linguistic nationalism of Plaid by getting it to accept both English and Welsh as national languages in Wales. He has promoted a Welsh Senate as the most feasible form of self-government for Wales (in the short run). And he has kept the party to constitutional, rather than illegal tactics, accepting English immigration despite the fear that this will undermine both the Welsh language and the prospects for independence.[11]

The future for the nationalist parties in Scotland and in Wales depends to a large extent on British voting behaviour, and on the attitude of British governments to Scotland and Wales. If English voters continue to support the Conservatives, while Scots and Welsh voters do not, this produces the election of Conservative governments whose legitimacy is questioned in Scotland and Wales. This is particularly the case when unpopular policies are pursued there. The potential for a revival in nationalism seems great, in these circumstances.

Notes

1. Since 1945, only two other Nationalist parties have contested elections: the Workers' Party of Scotland at the 1969 Glasgow Gorbals by-election (0.5 per cent of the vote), and Mudiad Gweriniaethol Cymru (Welsh Republican Movement) in 1950 at Ogmore (1.3 per cent of the vote). A 'Scottish Republican Socialist Party' was active in the eighties, with the aim of 'establishing a Scottish Workers' Socialist Republic' by revolutionary means, but it did not contest parliamentary elections. The 'Scottish Labour Party' founded in December 1975 and wound up in 1980, had two MPs, Jim Sillars and John Robertson, who defected from Labour because they considered that Labour's Scottish devolution proposals were too weak and had betrayed election promises. The SLP later moved to a more nationalist position, but was unable to keep its seats at the 1979 election, and put up only one other candidate. Sillars joined the SNP in 1980, when the SLP was disbanded.
2. The best general accounts of the SNP are Brand, J. (1978) *The National Movement in Scotland,* Routledge and Kegan Paul, and Mullin, W. A. R. (1979) 'The Scottish National Party', in H. M. Drucker (ed.) *Multi-Party Politics,* Macmillan. For Plaid Cymru, see Balsom, D. (1979) 'Plaid Cymru: the Welsh National Party', in

Drucker, op cit., and Osmond, J. (1985) *The National Question Again. Welsh Political Identity in the 1980s,* Gower.

3. For a development of this theme, see McAllister, I. (1982) 'United Kingdom nationalist parties: one nationalism or three?', in P. Madgwick and R. Rose (eds) *The Territorial Dimension in United Kingdom Politics,* Macmillan.

4. Other seats won by the SNP between 1945 and 1987 are Western Isles (1970–87); Aberdeenshire East, Argyll, Banffshire, Clackmannan and East Stirlingshire, Moray and Nairn (February 1974–9); Angus South, Dunbartonshire East, Galloway, Perth and East Perthshire (October 1974–9); Angus East, Banff and Buchan, Moray (1987–). The three seats won in 1987 were roughly the same as corresponding seats won in 1974 (Angus South, Banffshire, Aberdeenshire East, Moray and Nairn).

5. Miller, W. L., Sarlvik, B., Crewe, I. and Alt, J. (1977) 'The connection between SNP voting and the demand for Scottish self-government', *European Journal of Political Research,* Vol. 5, pp. 83–102, and Miller, W., Brand, J. and Jordan, M. (1980) *Oil and the Scottish Voter, 1974–79,* Social Science Research Council.

6. A fuller discussion of the organisation of the SNP and PC is given by Mullin and Balsom, op. cit. For the SNP, see also Levy, R. (1986) 'The search for a rational strategy: the Scottish National Party and devolution, 1974–79', *Political Studies,* Vol. XXXIV, No. 2, pp. 236–248.

7. Balsom, op. cit., p. 140.

8. Michels, R. (1911) *Political Parties. A Sociological Study of the Oligarchical Tendencies of Modern Democracy* (first German edn). Later English translation (1962), Collier Books.

9. Levy, op. cit.

10. Balsom, op. cit. p. 148.

11. Thomas, N. (1988) 'Can Plaid Cymru survive until 1994?', *Planet,* No. 70 (August/September), pp. 3–10.

Key dates

1925		Foundation of Plaid Cymru (Welsh National Party).
1928		Foundation of National Party of Scotland (in 1934 became Scottish National Party).
1966	July	Gwynfor Evans wins Carmarthen by-election for PC.
1967	Nov.	Winifred Ewing wins Hamilton by-election for SNP.
1974	Feb.	Seven SNP MPs and two PC MPs elected.
1974	Oct.	Eleven SNP MPs and three PC MPs elected.
1979	Mar.	Referendums on Scotland Act and Wales Act in Scotland and Wales. Scotland Act supported by 52 per cent to 48 per cent against, but fails to meet '40 per cent of electorate' requirement. Wales Act rejected by 80 per cent of those

voting. Later that month, SNP proposes Vote of No Confidence in Callaghan Government, after Callaghan refuses to put repeal of Scotland Act to early vote of the House of Commons. In subsequent Vote of No Confidence, proposed by the Conservatives, Callaghan Government defeated by one vote.

1979 May In general election, SNP and PC reduced to two MPs each (in 1983 election, these seats retained; in 1987 election each returns three MPs).

1988 Sept. SNP Conference supports non-payment of the community charge ('poll tax'), and 'Independence in Europe' policy.

Nov. Jim Sillars wins Govan by-election.

1989 Jan. SNP delegates pull out of planning meeting for Scottish Constitutional Convention.

10

British Political Parties in the 1980s

GILLIAN PEELE

Political parties are the life blood of a democracy. If they are vigorous and responsive to the changing features of the society, the political system as a whole will be healthy; if they are organisationally weak or incapable of adapting to new demands, they may damage confidence in the system as a whole. The eighties have seen a number of changes occurring in the organisation, strength and ideology of British parties and it is likely that the force of these changes will continue to be felt over the next decade. Before examining the nature of some of these changes, it is worth glancing backward to the state of the parties in the preceding decades in order to place the changes in the party system in context.

Until the early seventies there was a marked tone of complacency in the way scholars treated the party system and the relationship between the electorate and the parties on the one hand and between the parties and the wider constitutional system on the other. Robert McKenzie's classic work *British Political Parties* (first published in 1955) is a case in point. What is striking about McKenzie's study (apart from the extent to which events within the Labour Party since 1970 have contradicted his general thesis) is the somewhat uncritical tone and the broad assumption that Britain's two-party system (the Liberals rated only an appendix) had evolved to an admirable level of consensual stability.

Although McKenzie obviously recognised the difference in character between the Conservative and Labour Parties, it was a fundamental part of his argument that the constitutional imperatives of the parliamentary and cabinet systems would always minimise those differences in practice. Concern about the relative power of the parliamentary and extra-parliamentary elements in the Labour Party was unnecessary. 'Indeed' he wrote 'if the Labour Party had been as continually in office as the Conservatives have been, it is highly likely that the issue of the external control of the Parliamentary Party would be nearly as dead in the Labour Party as it is with the Conservatives.' Radical changes within the party system were not anticipated and were not deemed desirable since its logic fitted well with the broader framework of parliamentary democracy.

This period of complacency about our political parties came to a sudden end in the seventies. Inevitably the two major parties incurred some of the blame for the perceived crisis of governability associated with the Heath government and the subsequent periods of minority or near minority Labour government as well as for the problems of the British economy. The electorate's increasingly apparent disenchantment with the two-party system prompted renewed attention to be given to the possibility of electoral reform. The destruction of the simple plurality system, it was suggested, would have the effect both of providing fairer representation and of giving more stable government, since it would preclude the tendency for small shifts in opinion to lead to exaggerated movements in party support. The parties were thus seen as imperfect representatives of public opinion and as impediments to tackling the policy problems facing Britain. They were also criticised for creating a political climate in which partisan bickering displaced constructive policy appraisal. A number of these themes can be traced in the writings on parties in the seventies but perhaps the most characteristic is the trenchant essay by S. E. Finer in the 1975 symposium *Adversary Politics and Electoral Reform*.

Some of the features of British political behaviour which gave rise to these concerns about the party system in the seventies are still there in the eighties. On the other hand some developments are either quite new or were only barely foreseen in the seventies.

In examining the distinctive features of British parties in the eighties it is helpful to look at the issues under five headings.

Dealignment and electoral uncertainty

During the seventies the behaviour of the British electorate began to change fundamentally. Not merely did the two major parties' share of the vote drop significantly but there was increased volatility as voters switched their electoral preference. Survey evidence revealed a decline in the number of people who identified with a party. In addition, even when they did identify with a party, there was a decline in the degree of attachment felt by voters towards that party. The standard explanation for this behaviour was that Britain was experiencing a dealignment – a loosening of the bonds between voters and the party system, bonds formed on the basis of the major political cleavage in Britain: social class. Electoral change created a new environment for the parties since their competition for votes could no longer start with a number of the old assumptions about the proportion of people likely to shift their allegiance or about where the appeal of a particular party might be strongest.

The eighties have seen the continuation of electoral uncertainty, although there are now a number of competing explanations of what is actually happening in the electorate. According to one theory what has been happening is that dealignment has continued and voters, instead of voting in a semi-automatic manner on the basis of party identity as in the past, now make up their minds on the basis of issues. Obviously if this explanation were true, there would be an enormous premium not merely on having an attractive set of policies to put before the electorate but also on packaging those policies effectively. The role of party advertising and the media would be increasingly important.

A second explanation of the change which has occurred emphasises the extent to which a combination of changing party appeals and social change have laid the foundations for a new political alignment. Instead of the simple dichotomy between the manual and non-manual groups, account should be taken of a number of other divisions in the electorate. Thus for example there is a distinction between skilled manual workers and unskilled manual workers. The former group is more likely to be relatively affluent (especially in the South) and to identify much more with the middle class than with the traditional sectors of the working class. On this theory we have in the making a new alignment of forces in which Conservatives appeal to the expanding and affluent sections of society while Labour's appeal becomes concentrated in the declining areas and impoverished sections of the country.

Finally, there is an argument which suggests that, while it needs some modification, the traditional theory of party identification still offers the best account of voting behaviour. Underlying the British electorate's voting behaviour is still a basic partisan identity on this theory. Moreover, the partisan identity is still, on this theory, largely based on patterns of social and economic inequality. However, partisan identity does not equal votes and for a variety of reasons the Labour Party has been unable to get its natural supporters to vote for it. Poor leadership, unattractive policies and an extremist image have all produced a situation in which Labour has done artificially badly.

This theory does not underestimate the difficulty of returning a Labour government in the near future nor does it answer the question of whether a series of elections in which Labour under-performs does not weaken Labour's partisan support. What this theory does suggest, however, is that the causes of Labour's decline are remediable rather than the product of either a long-term realignment or a shift to a style of voting in which traditional class-based appeals have no place.

Debate will doubtless continue to surround these explanations of recent electoral change. In the meantime the parties have had to cope with the evident fluidity of electoral opinion and to learn to live in a world where much of the framework of assumptions about partisan choice has been challenged.

The structure of party competition

The most visible sign that British party politics was changing in the eighties was, of course, the formation of the Social Democratic Party in 1981 and its subsequent entry into an arrangement with the Liberal Party to form the Alliance. Although the arguments about merger which occurred after the 1987 election have weakened the strength of this third force, it did for a period threaten the two major parties' electoral dominance. And it forced a rethinking of some of the established conventions of party politics as well as leading to a good deal of speculation about such issues as tactical voting and hung Parliaments.

The history of the Social Democratic Party has revealed a number of interesting aspects of British party politics in the eighties. First, it is clear from the enthusiasm which the new party generated initially that there is still a substantial body of people anxious to become involved in active politics in Britain. Secondly, it showed how quickly the intellectual terrain was moving. The Gang of Four left the Labour Party because it had moved too far to the left, had repudiated European unity and had compromised the supremacy of the parliamentary party. Yet from the beginning, it was clear that the founders of the new party all had slightly different ideas about the role which the party should play in the political system and about its ideological orientation. It was one thing to reject certain developments inside the Labour Party; quite another to develop new and exciting policies for the fledgling party. The collapse of the Keynesian consensus had left social democracy without intellectual anchorage; the alliance with the Liberals produced new policy dilemmas especially over defence and the market economy.

The advent of the SDP did not by itself change the structure of party competition in Britain, although it did add another party organisation to those competing for power at the national level. The survival of the Liberals – albeit at times tenuously – illustrated that Britain was perhaps better described as a two-and-a-half-party system rather than as a pure two-party system. What the formation of the SDP did was to inject new resources and dynamism into the third force in British politics – to a point where there was much debate about whether the Alliance might in the long run replace Labour as the major opposition party.

The result of the 1987 elections in which the Alliance failed to overtake Labour in its share of the popular vote and the subsequent disputes within the SDP about merger with the Liberals have undermined the strength of the third force. But even if the impact of the new competition has been temporarily blunted it would be unwise for the two major parties to believe that they can ever again behave like the lazy duopolists of the fifties. Indeed, the elections to the European Parliament in 1989 underlined how quickly a new party can achieve prominence. For, although the Greens' performance gained them no seats, the Green Party did focus attention on environmental issues and seriously worried the other parties.

Conservative Party dominance

One of the concrete results of the growth of a third force in British politics was the continued success of the Conservative Party. Indeed some people, as a result of the 1987 election, were talking not so much of a two-party system or a two-and-a-half-party system but of a one-party dominant system.

Conservative success in 1979, in 1983 and in 1987 can be attributed to a number of factors, of which a split opposition vote is only one. More important in 1983 and 1987 was the Labour Party's continued failure to appeal to voters although the reasons were rather different in 1983 and 1987. In 1983 the campaign was a disaster and Foot's leadership was no less so. In 1987 the Labour Party still failed to make headway despite an attractive leader and a campaign which was thought by many to be the best organised of the three. It was the lack of credible policies and the general image of the extremist influence which destroyed Labour's chances.

Explanations of Conservative success which focus on Labour weakness or the split opposition vote are not sufficient to explain the Conservatives' remarkable political achievement. Credit must be given to Mrs Thatcher's leadership ability and the peculiar synthesis of free market and populist policies which she has expressed. Although it would be a mistake to exaggerate her intuitive understanding of what makes the British public tick (she has for example severely underestimated the support for good public services, especially in the health and educational sectors) she has captured perfectly certain basic desires such as home ownership.

The sustained period of Conservative government has enabled that party to set the political agenda in a way which has transformed party political debate. The crumbling of Keynesian consensus offered an opportunity for new thinking about the role of the state and best ways of providing services in modern Britain.

Initially it seemed that the Conservative programme might be dominated by economic concerns to the exclusion of other topics. In fact, however, the range of policies which has emerged is a very broad one and the party has been successful in linking its programme to imaginative themes likely to appeal to the electorate. Thus privatisation has been broadened from a remedy for the problem of state-owned industry to the much more general notion of popular capitalism, while the reforms of education have been presented in terms of the broader goal of freedom of choice.

The 1988 Conservative Party conference underlined the extent to which the Tories have been able to develop policies and themes which appear fresh and interesting. The emphasis on environmental issues and the concept of active citizenship were important ideas for the Conservatives since they allowed the party to answer those opponents who charged that the kind of society which Conservatives had created was a selfish and materialistic one.

Therefore, although the agenda of contemporary Conservatism remains radical and although concern to create a more dynamic, entrepreneurial society continues to give the party's ideology its cutting edge, there is a more evident awareness of the need to justify policies in moral and non-economic terms. And there is also an awareness of the limits of market forces in the process of policy reform. Thus, although it seemed that the tone of debate in right-wing circles might well lead to major reforms of the National Health Service, it now seems that a combination of administrative and political reasons have ruled any fundamental change out of court.

Whether a new consensus has emerged as a result of the three Thatcher election victories remains to be seen. My own view is that on trade union reform, on council house sales and on privatisation the government has already achieved a new consensus. With care – and the money to make it work – the government will probably be able to achieve a new educational consensus despite the opposition which greeted aspects of the 1988 Education Act. The Labour Party has now revised its policies to fit the new mood and the new approach to issues which the Conservative government has initiated. Labour's policy review, while fundamental and far-reaching in design, is unlikely to be able to be received with total enthusiasm within the party and the

Labour leadership will face an uphill struggle to keep the whole party in step behind the new policies.

The fragmentation of the Alliance after the 1987 election means that, although there will be policy initiatives developed as a response to the Conservative agenda, the political significance of these initiatives will be minimal. David Owen's attempts to force the SDP and the Liberals to develop distinctive social market policies are now likely to be subordinated to his efforts to preserve his organisation. The SLD for their part remain plagued by an identity crisis.

The Conservatives' advantage in political argument seems likely to continue until there is either a broad intellectual movement away from the conceptual framework within which modern Conservatism operates or a major shift which would make the opposition parties able to respond effectively to the electorate's demands. The antennae of the Conservative Party seem to be sufficiently sensitive, however, to pick up on any movements in public opinion and the likelihood of any such developments leaving the party stranded seems remote. The shock of losing seats in the European elections of 1989 forced a change of party character and the agile Kenneth Baker was placed in control at Central Office.

Party management

A fourth distinctive feature of British political parties in the eighties has been a debate – sometimes explicit, sometimes implicit – about what political parties should do in a modern society. Broadly speaking, many of the debates within the Labour Party and the Liberal Party have been the product of a greater demand from the rank and file to be able to participate not just in the peripheral aspects of the party's life but in the core functions of leadership selection and policy-making. The crusade for internal party democracy in the Labour Party has made leadership of the party extremely difficult and created an image of the party which the electorate has found unappealing. In addition Labour has had to cope with the Militant Tendency within its ranks and to find ways of handling demands from ethnic minorities for separate black sections and from local councillors anxious for support for resistance to budget cuts. The problem has not been simply the demand for internal party democracy but the combination of that demand with a climate in which a number of groups within the Labour constituency have developed specific issue agendas. The Labour leader has therefore been caught between the imperatives of national politics (responding to the new agenda) and the imperatives of party politics.

The Liberal Party has also developed its mechanisms of participation in the eighties – a trend which made its relationships with the much more centrist SDP inherently uneasy. Inevitably perhaps, parties which are out of power need to provide their activists with satisfaction and increasingly this has come to mean direct participation in the selection of the leader and policy participation.

The Conservative Party has not been greatly troubled by problems of internal management in the eighties but it has had to face the question of what its party organisation should be doing. In the aftermath of the 1987 election there was speculation in the press that Conservative Central Office ought to be geared more effectively to publicising government achievements and policy advocacy, presumably at the expense of anything that passed for political research. There has in addition been the problem of securing harmony between the outlook of Conservatives at Westminster and the outlook of Conservatives in the European Parliament and this problem may become worse as European issues impinge more on domestic politics. In 1988 there was a rumour that the European candidates' list was being purged of individuals considered too supportive of closer political integration between the countries of the European Community, and the 1988 party conference at Brighton witnessed a certain nervousness about a debate over European affairs. It is just possible that the MEPs with their own electorates and a different set of institutions to operate will prove far more difficult to manage on policy issues than any faction at Westminster.

New ways of winning elections

The final change in British party politics is perhaps the one with most long term significance. Certainly it is one of the least noticed. The 1987 campaign confirmed the absorption into British politics of a number of new ideas and strategies which promise to alter not merely the character of election campaigns but also the quality of political debate in Britain. Take first the role of the media. 1987 saw the triumph of the television-led campaign. Politicians appeal to voters not directly but indirectly via the television cameras. By this I do not mean simply that more people watch politicians on the box than ever see them live in their constituencies. It is rather that every event of a tightly-scheduled election programme is geared to maximising the effect of television and making a maximum amount of impact for the morning newspapers. The media no longer report politicians. Politicians and the media are interlocked in a performance in which the electorate is as irrelevant to the movement as the audience watching a *pas-de-deux* at a ballet.

Behind the impact of the television cameras on the election directly there is, of course, the broader question of opinion formation between campaigns. The concentration of ownership in the newspaper industry and the overwhelming Conservative sympathy of the press means that it is to television that opposition parties must look for a fair coverage of their case. Allegations of bias against the BBC from the Conservative Party reflect an appreciation of the impact of television on the presentation of issues. Yet the world in which the airwaves were shared between two major operators has already passed and will soon give way to a much more pluralistic and competitive television environment. In these circumstances it is likely that the kind of television journalism practised by the BBC and existing independent companies will become minority viewing. Whether the emergence of a more competitive television universe will produce the kinds of concentration of ownership that have evolved in the press remains to be seen; but it is at least a possibility that some of the developments experienced in relation to the uniformity of opinion in the press will occur in television.

A second change of enormous but as yet still developing importance is the use of advertising agents to plan strategy. The 1987 campaign was followed by a number of candid inquests. These inquests highlighted the role attached to advertising agencies and an increasing emphasis on selling politics. Nor was this development confined to the campaign itself. Saatchi and Saatchi (the agency which handled the Conservative campaign) did not

merely devise the theme for the 1986 Conservative Party conference but also helped draft ministers' speeches to that conference
in line with the message. It may be that Conservative Party
conferences have always been so bland that manipulating them in
this way is not a serious loss to the democratic process. On the
other hand, the subordination of the central event in a party's
calendar to the dynamics of designer politics is surely cause for
some concern. Certainly some expressions of resentment surfaced
during the 1988 Conservative Party conference as it became clear
that Northern Ireland would be kept off the conference agenda.
And during the law and order debate – which is a perennial
opportunity to advocate tougher policies than the government
believes acceptable – one speaker took advantage of the micro-
phone to hold a snap 'referendum' on hanging against the wishes
of the platform. However, such episodes can be dismissed as
publicity stunts and do little to disturb the image of a profession-
ally organised and united party.

Traditional political activity at the grassroots level is also likely
to be transformed by the advent of cheap computers and direct
mail. Thus far direct mail has not been fully exploited in British
politics, though the Conservatives and the SDP have made some
significant use of it in fund-raising.

Cumulatively these developments have created a very different
environment for Britain's political parties than that which existed
in the sixties. If that environment seems in some respects to
trivialise and cheapen politics, in other respects it points towards
a more open and exciting style of party competition than before.
Whether all the parties can respond to those changes with equal
flexibility remains to be seen. But it would be a mistake to believe
that they will be easily reversed.

Appendix: General Election Results Since 1945

Table 1 1945

	Conservative	Labour	Liberal	Other	Total
Seats					
At dissolution	398	166	18	33	615
After election	213	393	12	22	640
Votes					
Percentage of total	39.8	48.3	9.1	2.8	
Change since 1935	−13.9	+10.4	+2.7	+0.8	

Labour overall majority of 146. Turnout 73.3 per cent.

Table 2 1950

	Conservative	Labour	Liberal	Other	Total
Seats					
At dissolution	218	391	10	21	640
After election	298	315	9	9	625
Votes					
Percentage of total	43.5	46.1	9.1	1.3	
Change since 1945	+3.7	−2.2	+0.1	−1.4	

Labour overall majority of 5. Turnout 84 per cent.

Table 3 1951

	Conservative	Labour	Liberal	Other	Total
Seats					
At dissolution	298	314	4	2	625
After election	321	295	6	3	625
Votes					
Percentage of total	48.0	48.8	2.5	0.7	
Change since 1950	+4.5	+2.7	−6.6	−0.6	

Conservative overall majority of 17. Turnout 82.5 per cent.

Table 4 1955

	Conservative	Labour	Liberal	Other	Total
Seats					
At dissolution	322	294	6	3	625
After election	344	277	6	3	630
Votes					
Percentage of total	49.7	46.4	2.7	1.2	
Change since 1951	+1.7	−2.4	+0.2	+0.5	

Conservative overall majority of 58. Turnout 78.7 per cent.

Table 5 1959

	Conservative	Labour	Liberal	Other	Total
Seats					
At dissolution	342	281	6	1	630
After election	365	258	6	1	630
Votes					
Percentage of total	49.4	43.8	5.9	0.9	
Change since 1955	−0.3	−2.6	+3.2	−0.2	

Conservative overall majority of 100. Turnout 78.8 per cent.

Table 6 1964

	Conservative	Labour	Liberal	Other	Total
Seats					
At dissolution	360	262	7	2	630
After election	304	317	9	−	630
Votes					
Percentage of total	43.4	44.1	11.2	1.3	
Change since 1959	−6.0	−0.3	+5.3	+0.4	

Labour overall majority of 4. Turnout 77.1 per cent.

Table 7 1966

	Conservative	Labour	Liberal	Other	Total
Seats					
At dissolution	304	316	10	–	630
After election	253	363	12	2	630
Votes					
Percentage of total	41.9	47.9	8.5	1.7	
Change since 1964	−1.5	+3.8	−2.7	0.4	

Labour overall majority of 96. Turnout 75.8 per cent.

Table 8 1970

	Conservative	Labour	Liberal	Other	Total
Seats					
At dissolution	264	346	13	7	630
After election	330	287	6	7	630
Votes					
Percentage of total	46.4	43.0	7.5	3.1	
Change since 1966	+4.3	−4.9	−1.0	+1.4	

Conservative overall majority of 30. Turnout 72 per cent.

Table 9 February 1974

	Conservative	Labour	Liberal	Other	Total
Seats					
At dissolution	323	287	11	9	630
After election	297	301	14	23	635
Votes					
Percentage of total	37.9	37.1	19.3	5.7	
Change since 1970	−6.5	−5.9	+11.8	+2.6	

No overall majority. Turnout 78.8 per cent.

Table 10 October 1974

	Conservative	Labour	Liberal	Other	Total
Seats					
At dissolution	297	300	15	23	635
After election	277	319	13	26	635
Votes					
Percentage of total	35.8	39.2	18.3	6.7	
Change since Feb. 1974	−2.1	+2.1	−1.0	+1.0	

Labour overall majority of 3. Turnout 72.8 per cent.

Table 11 1979

	Conservative	Labour	Liberal	Other	Total
Seats					
At dissolution	284	309	14	28	635
After election	339	269	11	16	635
Votes					
Percentage of total	43.9	36.9	13.8	5.4	
Change since Oct. 1974	+8.1	−2.3	−4.5	−1.3	

Conservative overall majority of 43. Turnout 76.0 per cent.

Table 12 1983

	Conservative	Labour	Liberal	Other	Total
Seats					
At dissolution	336	240	42	17	635
After election	397	209	23	21	650
Votes					
Percentage of total	42.4	27.6	25.4	4.6	
Change since 1979	−1.5	−9.3	+11.6	−0.8	

Conservative overall majority of 144. Turnout 72.7 per cent.

Table 13 1987

	Conservative	Labour	Liberal	Other	Total
Seats					
At dissolution	393	208	27	22	650
After election	376	229	22	23	650
Votes					
Percentage of total	42.2	30.8	22.6	4.4	
Change since 1983	−0.2	+3.2	−2.8	−0.2	

Conservative overall majority of 102. Turnout 75.3 per cent.

Index

153